The Huge Book of Unbelievable Facts

by
Jake Jacobs

* * * * *

Published by Jake Jacobs

1.

Francis Lightfoot Lee was born on October 14, 1734, in Stratford, Virginia.

2.

He was the fourth son of Thomas Lee and Hannah Ludwell Lee, a prominent Virginia family.

3.

Lee received his education at the College of William & Mary and studied law under his brother Richard Henry Lee.

4.

He served as a Justice of the Peace and a member of the Virginia House of Burgesses.

5.

Lee was a staunch advocate for colonial rights and a critic of British policies, which eventually led to the American Revolution.

6.

In 1774, Lee was elected to the First Continental Congress, where he represented Virginia alongside his brother Richard Henry Lee.

7.

He was known for his eloquence and passionate speeches defending colonial rights and advocating for independence from Britain.

8.

Lee signed the Declaration of Independence on July 4, 1776, as a representative of Virginia.

9.

During the Revolutionary War, Lee served as a member of the Virginia State Senate and the Continental Congress.

10.

He actively supported the war effort, providing financial assistance and supplies to the Continental Army.

11.

Lee was involved in drafting the Articles of Confederation, the first governing document of the United States.

12.

He opposed the ratification of the United States Constitution and believed it granted too much power to the federal government.

13.

Lee retired from politics in 1792 and focused on his agricultural pursuits at his plantation in Richmond County, Virginia.

14.

He was an avid farmer and experimented with new agricultural techniques and crops.

15.

Lee was a proponent of religious freedom and supported the disestablishment of the Anglican Church in Virginia.

16.

He advocated for the separation of church and state and the protection of religious liberties.

17.

Lee was known for his wit, intelligence, and refined manners, which made him a respected figure among his peers.

18.

He was a close friend and correspondent of Thomas Jefferson, with whom he shared political ideals and philosophical discussions.

19.

Lee was married to Rebecca Plater Tayloe, with whom he had six children.

20.

He was a strong advocate for the abolition of slavery and worked towards its gradual elimination in Virginia.

21.

Lee played a significant role in shaping the Virginia Constitution of 1776, which established the state's government during the Revolutionary War.

22.

He was appointed to the Board of War, where he provided oversight and guidance to the military operations of the Continental Army.

23.

Lee served as a delegate to the Virginia Constitutional Convention in 1788, where he continued to voice concerns about the power of the federal government.

24.

He supported the adoption of the Bill of Rights as a safeguard for individual liberties.

25.

Lee participated in the Virginia Convention of 1776, which declared independence from Great Britain and established Virginia as a sovereign state.

42.

He was appointed to various committees, including the Committee of Correspondence and the Committee of Safety, which played crucial roles in organizing resistance to British rule.

43.

Lee supported the idea of a strong state government and was an advocate for states' rights throughout his political career.

44.

He played a significant role in shaping Virginia's political landscape and influencing the development of its laws and institutions.

45.

Lee's commitment to liberty and individual rights made him a revered figure among the American colonists.

46.

He believed in the power of the people and the importance of their active participation in shaping their government.

47.

Lee's writings and speeches provided intellectual and philosophical foundations for the American Revolution and influenced the drafting of the Declaration of Independence.

48.

He played a crucial role in mobilizing public support for the cause of independence and rallying the colonists against British oppression.

49.

Lee's legacy as a founding father of the United States is celebrated for his unwavering commitment to the principles of freedom, justice, and self-governance.

50.

His contributions to the early years of the nation laid the groundwork for the democratic ideals that continue to shape American society today.

51.

Richard Henry Lee was born on January 20, 1732, in Westmoreland County, Virginia.

52.

He came from a prominent Virginia family, known for its influential members in politics and law.

53.

Lee received his education in England and returned to Virginia to pursue a career in law.

54.

He served as a justice of the peace and later as a member of the Virginia House of Burgesses.

55.

Lee was an early advocate for colonial rights and a vocal critic of British policies that infringed upon those rights.

56.

In 1774, Lee was elected to the First Continental Congress, where he represented Virginia alongside his brother, Francis Lightfoot Lee.

57.

Lee was a powerful orator and delivered passionate speeches defending colonial rights and advocating for independence from Britain.

58.

He introduced the resolution for independence in the Second Continental Congress on June 7, 1776.

59.

Lee signed the Declaration of Independence on July 4, 1776, as a representative of Virginia.

60.

Lee played a crucial role in shaping the early years of the American Revolution and in securing foreign support for the American cause.

61.

He was instrumental in forging alliances with European powers, such as France, to aid the American colonies in their fight against Britain.

62.

Lee served as the President of the Continental Congress in 1784.

63.

He was a strong proponent of states' rights and advocated for a decentralized government with limited federal power.

64.

Lee was one of the primary authors of the Articles of Confederation, the first governing document of the United States.

65.

He believed in the importance of individual liberty and played a significant role in drafting the Virginia Declaration of Rights, a precursor to the Bill of Rights.

66.

Lee served as a U.S. Senator from Virginia from 1789 to 1792.

67.

He was an active participant in shaping the new federal government and supported the adoption of the United States Constitution.

68.

Lee played a crucial role in the negotiations that led to the location of the nation's capital in Washington, D.C.

69.

He opposed the ratification of the Jay Treaty with Great Britain, arguing that it compromised American sovereignty.

70.

Lee was a vocal opponent of slavery and advocated for its abolition, although he himself owned slaves.

71.

He believed in the power of education and promoted the establishment of public schools in Virginia.

72.

Lee was a strong advocate for religious freedom and supported the disestablishment of the Anglican Church in Virginia.

73.

He was a close friend and correspondent of other Founding Fathers, such as Thomas Jefferson and George Washington.

74.

Lee's political career was marked by his commitment to republican ideals and his efforts to protect the rights and liberties of the American people.

75.

He retired from politics in 1792 and returned to his plantation, where he focused on agriculture and writing.

76.

Lee authored several influential political and historical works, including "Letters from the Federal Farmer" and "Memoir of the Life of Richard Henry Lee."

77.

He was a proponent of agricultural innovation and introduced new farming methods on his plantation.

78.

Lee was an active member of the Freemasons and held leadership positions within the organization.

79.

He supported the creation of the Library of Congress and donated his personal library to help establish it.

80.

Lee's advocacy for individual rights and limited government laid the foundation for the American political system.

81.

He played a significant role in shaping Virginia's political landscape and influenced the state's constitution and laws.

82.

Lee's commitment to republican principles and his contributions to the cause of independence earned him the nickname "Cicero of the Revolution."

83.

He was a key figure in the formation of the Democratic-Republican Party, which championed states' rights and strict construction of the Constitution.

84.

Lee was a strong advocate for the protection of private property rights and believed in the importance of economic freedom.

85.

He supported the development of American industry and was involved in various business ventures, including iron production and trade.

86.

Lee's tireless efforts to secure foreign aid during the Revolutionary War helped turn the tide in favor of the American colonies.

87.

He was elected as a delegate to the Virginia Ratifying Convention in 1788, where he argued in favor of ratifying the Constitution.

88.

Lee's political career spanned over four decades, during which he consistently fought for the principles of liberty and self-governance.

89.

He was known for his eloquence and rhetorical skills, which made him a powerful advocate for the American cause.

90.

Lee's commitment to public service and his dedication to the ideals of the American Revolution earned him the respect and admiration of his peers.

91.

He was an influential figure in Virginia politics and helped shape the state's early government.

92.

Lee's speeches and writings continue to be studied and revered for their insight into the principles of liberty and republicanism.

93.

He believed in the importance of civic virtue and public participation in the democratic process.

94.

Lee's contributions to the founding of the United States were instrumental in shaping the nation's early development and its political principles.

95.

He advocated for a strong national government that protected individual rights and promoted the general welfare.

96.

Lee's political philosophy was rooted in the Enlightenment ideals of reason, liberty, and equality.

97.

He was a staunch defender of the principles laid out in the
Declaration of Independence and fought tirelessly for their
realization.

98.

Lee's legacy as a Founding Father and statesman is celebrated for his
unwavering commitment to the cause of freedom and his dedication
to public service.

99.

His contributions to American history continue to be remembered
and honored, and his ideas and principles remain influential to this
day.

100.

Lee's life and career serve as a testament to the courage and vision of
the men and women who fought for the birth of the United States
and laid the foundation for a new nation.

101.

The Atlantic puffin, also known as the common puffin, is a seabird
species found in the North Atlantic Ocean.

102.

Puffins have a distinctive appearance with their colorful beak, bright
orange legs, and black and white plumage.

103.

They are small birds, measuring about 25-30 centimeters in length
and weighing around 400-600 grams.

104.

Puffins are excellent divers and can plunge into the water to catch
fish at depths of up to 60 meters.

105.

They are known for their incredible flying abilities, with a wingspan of around 50-60 centimeters that allows them to glide through the air.

106.

Puffins have a unique way of holding fish in their beaks, with several spiny projections on their tongues that help them grip the slippery prey.

107.

These birds are highly social and often form large breeding colonies, known as puffin colonies or puffinries, on coastal cliffs and islands.

108.

Puffins are monogamous and usually mate for life, returning to the same nesting site each year.

109.

They are excellent burrowers and typically nest in deep burrows in the soil or in rocky crevices.

110.

Puffins lay a single egg each year, which both parents take turns incubating for about 40-45 days.

111.

The chicks, known as pufflings, are born covered in gray down feathers and are cared for by both parents until they fledge.

112.

Puffins primarily feed on small fish, such as herring, sand eels, and capelin, which they catch by diving underwater.

113.

They have specialized beaks that are well-suited for holding and carrying multiple fish at once.

114.

Puffins are known for their adorable and comical appearance, often referred to as "clowns of the sea" or "sea parrots."

115.

They are skilled swimmers and use their wings to "fly" underwater, propelling themselves with their webbed feet.

116.

Puffins have a unique way of cooling themselves in warm weather by panting, similar to dogs.

117.

These birds have excellent eyesight and can spot prey from great distances while flying.

118.

Puffins are migratory birds and spend the winter at sea, often far from land.

119.

They have a lifespan of around 20-25 years in the wild.

120.

Puffins have a strong homing instinct and can navigate back to their breeding grounds accurately, even after spending months at sea.

121.

They are found in several regions across the North Atlantic, including Iceland, Norway, the Faroe Islands, the United Kingdom, and parts of North America.

122.

Puffins are highly regarded as an iconic symbol of coastal wildlife and are popular among birdwatchers and nature enthusiasts.

123.

They are protected in many countries and are considered a species of conservation concern due to habitat loss and climate change.

124.

Puffins play a vital role in marine ecosystems by controlling fish populations and redistributing nutrients through their guano.

125.

These birds have a unique vocalization, producing a series of low grunts and growls.

126.

Puffins are known to be social birds and engage in various displays and behaviors, such as bill tapping, head shaking, and courtship rituals.

127.

The beak of a puffin changes color during the breeding season, becoming brighter and more vibrant.

128.

Puffins are known to return to the same burrow each year and often maintain long-term partnerships with their breeding mates.

129.

They are excellent swimmers but struggle to take flight from the water, often needing a running start by flapping their wings rapidly.

130.

Puffins have a layered plumage that provides insulation and keeps them warm in cold waters.

131.

They have a high metabolic rate and require a significant amount of food each day to sustain their energy levels.

132.

Puffins are vulnerable to predation from larger seabirds, such as gulls and skuas, as well as mammalian predators like foxes and rats.

133.

These birds have a unique courtship display, known as the "billing" or "clowning" display, where they rub their beaks together.

134.

Puffins are skilled fliers, capable of reaching speeds of up to 55 miles per hour.

135.

They are highly adaptable and can adjust their diet and feeding behavior based on the availability of prey.

136.

Puffins have a specialized gland located above their eye, known as the "pectoral gland," which secretes an oil-like substance that helps waterproof their feathers.

137.

They have a relatively low reproductive rate, with females typically laying only one egg per year.

138.

Puffins have a close relationship with their nesting colonies and often return to the same location where they were hatched.

139.

They are known for their agility in the air, with the ability to perform tight turns and acrobatic maneuvers.

140.

Puffins are sensitive to disturbances at their breeding sites and can be easily disturbed or frightened away.

141.

These birds have a keen sense of smell and can detect the scent of their burrow or nesting site.

142.

Puffins are known to engage in mutual preening, where they groom each other's feathers as a form of social bonding.

143.

They have an interesting digestive system that allows them to store and transport large quantities of fish in their stomachs to feed their chicks.

144.

Puffins are diurnal, meaning they are active during the day and rest or sleep at night.

145.

They have a streamlined body shape that reduces drag and allows
them to move swiftly through the water.

146.

Puffins are excellent divers and can stay underwater for up to a
minute while foraging.

147.

They have a unique ability to close their nostrils and create a
watertight seal while diving.

148.

Puffins are capable of traveling long distances in search of food,
sometimes covering hundreds of miles in a single foraging trip.

149.

They have a dense population in certain regions, with colonies
numbering in the tens of thousands of individuals.

150.

Puffins have a charismatic and charming presence, capturing the
hearts of people around the world with their adorable appearance and
fascinating behaviors.

151.

Atlantic spotted dolphins (Stenella frontalis) are a species of dolphin
found in the warm tropical and subtropical waters of the Atlantic
Ocean.

152.

They are medium-sized dolphins, measuring between 1.8 and 2.4
meters in length and weighing around 100 to 140 kilograms.

153.

Atlantic spotted dolphins have a distinct appearance, with a dark gray to black back, a lighter gray belly, and a prominent pattern of spots and speckles covering their bodies.

154.

The spots on their bodies can vary in color, ranging from light gray to tan or even pinkish hues.

155.

These dolphins are highly social and often found in large groups called pods, which can consist of hundreds or even thousands of individuals.

156.

They are known for their acrobatic behavior, frequently leaping out of the water, riding the bow waves of boats, and performing aerial flips and spins.

157.

Atlantic spotted dolphins are highly vocal and communicate using a variety of clicks, whistles, and other sounds.

158.

They have a lifespan of about 40 to 50 years in the wild.

159.

Atlantic spotted dolphins are opportunistic feeders, consuming a diverse diet that includes fish, squid, and crustaceans.

160.

They are skilled hunters and use coordinated strategies to herd and catch schools of fish.

161.

These dolphins are known to engage in cooperative hunting, where they work together to encircle and capture their prey.

162.

Atlantic spotted dolphins have been observed interacting with other dolphin species, such as bottlenose dolphins and common dolphins, forming mixed-species groups.

163.

They are known to be curious and playful, often approaching boats and swimmers to investigate their surroundings.

164.

Atlantic spotted dolphins have been observed riding the bow waves and wake of boats, exhibiting a behavior known as bow-riding.

165.

They are fast swimmers and can reach speeds of up to 37 kilometers per hour.

166.

Atlantic spotted dolphins are migratory and can travel long distances in search of food and suitable breeding grounds.

167.

They are found in various regions of the Atlantic Ocean, including the Gulf of Mexico, the Caribbean Sea, and the western coast of Africa.

168.

These dolphins are known for their energetic and social interactions, frequently engaging in leaping, tail slapping, and other playful behaviors.

169.

Atlantic spotted dolphins have a complex social structure, with distinct matrilineal groups consisting of related females and their offspring.

170.

Male dolphins often form bachelor groups or roam solitary, joining female groups during the mating season.

171.

The mating season for Atlantic spotted dolphins typically occurs in the spring and summer.

172.

The gestation period for females is around 11 months, after which a single calf is born.

173.

Calves are typically around 90 to 100 centimeters in length and weigh around 11 to 18 kilograms at birth.

174.

The mother provides care and protection to the calf, nursing it with milk for about 1 to 2 years.

175.

Atlantic spotted dolphins have been known to exhibit altruistic behavior, such as assisting injured or sick individuals.

176.

They are highly intelligent animals and have demonstrated problem-solving abilities and social learning.

177.

Atlantic spotted dolphins are vulnerable to various threats, including habitat loss, pollution, entanglement in fishing gear, and human disturbance.

178.

Conservation efforts are in place to protect these dolphins, including the establishment of marine protected areas and regulations to minimize human impacts.

179.

Researchers study Atlantic spotted dolphins to better understand their behavior, social structure, and population dynamics.

180.

These dolphins are known for their remarkable underwater agility, often performing tight turns and twists while swimming.

181.

Atlantic spotted dolphins have been observed engaging in "porpoising," where they swim rapidly, breaking the surface of the water in a series of leaps.

182.

They have a streamlined body shape, with a curved dorsal fin and a tapered tail that enables efficient swimming.

183.

These dolphins have excellent eyesight and hearing, allowing them to navigate their environment and locate prey.

184.

Atlantic spotted dolphins have a complex vocal repertoire, with individual dolphins having unique signature whistles that help them identify each other.

185.

They are known to exhibit a behavior called "strand feeding," where they herd fish towards shallow waters and then rush onto the beach to feed on them.

186.

Atlantic spotted dolphins have been observed using sponges as tools, holding them in their mouths while foraging on the seafloor to protect their sensitive snouts.

187.

They are highly adaptable to their environment and can adjust their feeding behavior and prey preferences based on availability.

188.

Atlantic spotted dolphins are susceptible to noise pollution, which can disrupt their communication and foraging activities.

189.

They have a dense blubber layer that helps them maintain body temperature in cold waters.

190.

Atlantic spotted dolphins are known to exhibit curiosity towards humans and have been observed approaching divers and interacting with them.

191.

These dolphins are known for their intricate and playful courtship displays, which can involve chasing, flipping, and touching.

192.

They have a complex social hierarchy within their pods, with dominant individuals having priority access to resources.

193.

Atlantic spotted dolphins are sometimes targeted by fisheries for human consumption, although the scale of this activity is relatively limited.

194.

They have been featured in various forms of media, including movies, documentaries, and wildlife photography.

195.

Atlantic spotted dolphins are important indicators of the overall health and biodiversity of marine ecosystems.

196.

They play a crucial role in the food chain, helping to control the populations of their prey species.

197.

These dolphins are a source of ecotourism in certain regions, attracting visitors who are interested in observing and learning about marine wildlife.

198.

Atlantic spotted dolphins are protected under national and international regulations, such as the Marine Mammal Protection Act and the Convention on International Trade in Endangered Species (CITES).

199.

They are considered a species of least concern on the IUCN Red List, indicating that their population is relatively stable.

200.

The study and conservation of Atlantic spotted dolphins contribute to our understanding of marine ecosystems and the importance of protecting the oceans for future generations.

201.

Gambell is a small community located on St. Lawrence Island in the Bering Sea, off the western coast of Alaska.

202.

The Gambell Sites refer to a collection of archaeological sites found in and around the village of Gambell.

203.

These sites have been inhabited for thousands of years, with evidence of human presence dating back at least 2,000 years.

204.

Gambell is home to the St. Lawrence Island Yupik people, who have a rich cultural heritage and deep connection to the land.

205.

The Gambell Sites provide valuable insights into the history, culture, and subsistence practices of the St. Lawrence Island Yupik people.

206.

The sites include archaeological features such as house pits, storage pits, ceremonial structures, and ancient trash deposits known as middens.

207.

Excavations at the Gambell Sites have revealed a wide range of artifacts, including tools, pottery fragments, bone and antler tools, and hunting implements.

208.

The artifacts found at the Gambell Sites provide important clues about the technology, craftsmanship, and daily life of the ancient inhabitants.

209.

The Gambell Sites are considered significant not only for their archaeological value but also for their cultural and spiritual importance to the St. Lawrence Island Yupik people.

210.

Traditional practices and knowledge are still passed down through generations in Gambell, and the sites serve as a connection to their ancestral heritage.

211.

The Gambell Sites are part of a broader cultural landscape that includes other archaeological sites, traditional hunting and fishing grounds, and sacred places.

212.

The St. Lawrence Island Yupik people have a deep respect for the land and the resources it provides, and their traditional subsistence practices are closely tied to the Gambell Sites.

213.

The sites are also important for understanding the environmental changes that have occurred in the region over time, including shifts in sea ice patterns and wildlife populations.

214.

Gambell is located in a region that is rich in marine resources, and the archaeological sites provide evidence of the long history of maritime subsistence practices.

215.

The St. Lawrence Island Yupik people have a strong connection to the sea and rely on fishing, hunting seals and whales, and gathering marine resources for their sustenance.

216.

The Gambell Sites have attracted the attention of archaeologists, anthropologists, and researchers from around the world who are interested in studying the unique cultural and historical aspects of the St. Lawrence Island Yupik people.

217.

Traditional storytelling and oral history are an integral part of the cultural heritage of the St. Lawrence Island Yupik people, and the Gambell Sites contribute to these narratives.

218.

The sites serve as a reminder of the resilience and adaptability of the St. Lawrence Island Yupik people, who have maintained their cultural traditions despite significant changes over the centuries.

219.

Gambell is also known for its rich birdlife, and the sites provide important nesting and breeding grounds for various seabird species.

220.

The Gambell Sites offer opportunities for community engagement, cultural preservation, and tourism, as visitors can learn about the history and traditions of the St. Lawrence Island Yupik people.

221.

The preservation and protection of the Gambell Sites are essential to maintain the integrity of the cultural landscape and ensure the continuation of traditional practices.

222.

The Gambell Sites are subject to ongoing research and documentation, with new discoveries and insights emerging as technology and methods improve.

223.

The sites are part of a broader effort to recognize and protect indigenous cultural heritage and promote collaboration between indigenous communities and researchers.

224.

Gambell has a strong sense of community and pride in its cultural heritage, and the preservation of the Gambell Sites is seen as a collective responsibility.

225.

The St. Lawrence Island Yupik people continue to maintain a strong connection to their ancestral lands, and the Gambell Sites are a physical manifestation of this connection.

226.

The Gambell Sites have provided valuable information about the prehistoric use of resources, such as the hunting of migratory marine mammals and the gathering of marine plants.

227.

The sites offer insights into the social organization and settlement patterns of the St. Lawrence Island Yupik people, including the development of permanent and seasonal settlements.

228.

The Gambell Sites have been a source of inspiration for contemporary artists, who draw on the rich cultural heritage of the St. Lawrence Island Yupik people in their work.

229.

The sites are a testament to the ingenuity and resourcefulness of the St. Lawrence Island Yupik people, who have adapted their subsistence practices to the challenging Arctic environment.

230.

The Gambell Sites are an important educational resource, providing opportunities for local youth to learn about their cultural heritage and engage in archaeological research.

231.

The sites have also contributed to the understanding of human migration patterns and the peopling of the Americas, as they are located in a region that played a significant role in early human dispersal.

232.

The Gambell Sites have been recognized as significant cultural properties by the State of Alaska and the federal government, highlighting their importance for preserving indigenous history and heritage.

233.

The sites have served as a focal point for cultural events, celebrations, and ceremonies, bringing the community together and reinforcing a sense of identity and belonging.

234.

The Gambell Sites are part of a broader effort to promote cultural tourism and sustainable development in the region, providing economic opportunities while preserving the cultural integrity of the community.

235.

The St. Lawrence Island Yupik people have a deep spiritual connection to the land and the natural world, and the Gambell Sites are considered sacred places where they can connect with their ancestors and the spirits.

236.

The sites have provided evidence of long-distance trade and interaction between different indigenous groups, highlighting the interconnectedness of ancient societies in the Arctic.

237.

The Gambell Sites have been the subject of interdisciplinary research, combining archaeological methods with oral history, ethnographic studies, and ecological research to provide a holistic understanding of the cultural landscape.

238.

The sites have contributed to the documentation and preservation of endangered languages, as the St. Lawrence Island Yupik people continue to pass down their traditional knowledge and language to younger generations.

239.

The Gambell Sites have been a source of inspiration for cultural revitalization efforts, including language revitalization programs, traditional arts and crafts, and community-based initiatives.

240.

The sites have provided insights into the technological advancements of the St. Lawrence Island Yupik people, including the development of specialized tools and techniques for hunting, fishing, and processing resources.

241.

The Gambell Sites have been used as outdoor classrooms, where community members and researchers collaborate to teach traditional knowledge, archaeology, and environmental science.

242.

The sites are also a reminder of the challenges faced by indigenous communities, including the impacts of colonialism, forced assimilation, and the loss of traditional lands.

243.

The Gambell Sites have been featured in documentaries, publications, and exhibitions, increasing public awareness and appreciation of the cultural heritage of the St. Lawrence Island Yupik people.

244.

The sites serve as a reminder of the long and continuous occupation of the St. Lawrence Island by indigenous peoples, challenging misconceptions about the "pristine" Arctic wilderness.

245.

The Gambell Sites have inspired cultural exchange programs and collaborations between the St. Lawrence Island Yupik people and other indigenous communities around the world.

246.

The sites have provided evidence of the artistic expressions of the St. Lawrence Island Yupik people, including carvings, sculptures, and decorative objects made from bone, ivory, and other materials.

247.

The Gambell Sites have been impacted by climate change, as rising temperatures, thawing permafrost, and coastal erosion pose significant challenges to the preservation of the cultural heritage.

248.

The sites have contributed to the understanding of traditional ecological knowledge and the sustainable management of natural resources in the Arctic.

249.

The Gambell Sites have played a role in the repatriation of ancestral remains and cultural artifacts, as the St. Lawrence Island Yupik people work towards reclaiming and preserving their heritage.

250.

The sites symbolize the resilience and strength of the St. Lawrence Island Yupik people, who have preserved their cultural traditions and adapted to changing circumstances while maintaining a deep connection to their ancestral lands.

251.

Sourdough Lodge is a historic lodge located in the heart of the wilderness, offering a unique and rustic experience for visitors.

252.

The lodge is situated in a picturesque setting, surrounded by towering trees, scenic mountains, and pristine lakes.

253.

The lodge is known for its warm and welcoming atmosphere, providing a cozy retreat for travelers seeking a peaceful getaway.

254.

Sourdough Lodge has a rich history dating back several decades, with stories and anecdotes that contribute to its charm and character.

255.

The lodge's architecture and interior design reflect a traditional rustic style, incorporating natural materials such as wood and stone.

256.

Sourdough Lodge offers a range of accommodation options, from private cabins to comfortable rooms, catering to different preferences and group sizes.

257.

The lodge is known for its exceptional hospitality, with friendly staff who go above and beyond to ensure a memorable stay for guests.

258.

Sourdough Lodge provides a variety of amenities to enhance the guest experience, including a cozy lounge area, a restaurant serving delicious local cuisine, and outdoor recreational facilities.

259.

The lodge is a haven for outdoor enthusiasts, offering easy access to hiking trails, fishing spots, and wildlife viewing opportunities.

260.

Sourdough Lodge is a popular destination for photographers, with stunning landscapes and abundant wildlife providing endless photo opportunities.

261.

The lodge organizes guided tours and activities, allowing guests to explore the surrounding wilderness and learn about the local flora, fauna, and cultural heritage.

262.

Sourdough Lodge is committed to sustainability and eco-friendly practices, implementing measures to minimize its environmental impact and support conservation efforts.

263.

The lodge is a great place for birdwatching, as the surrounding area is home to a diverse range of bird species, including migratory birds.

264.

Sourdough Lodge offers a chance to disconnect from the hustle and bustle of everyday life, providing a peaceful and rejuvenating environment.

265.

The lodge is located near scenic water bodies, offering opportunities for boating, kayaking, and canoeing.

266.

Sourdough Lodge hosts occasional live music performances and cultural events, showcasing local talent and adding to the vibrant atmosphere.

267.

The lodge is a pet-friendly establishment, allowing guests to bring their furry friends along for a memorable vacation.

268.

Sourdough Lodge is a gateway to nearby national parks and wilderness areas, making it an ideal basecamp for outdoor adventures.

269.

The lodge is equipped with modern amenities such as Wi-Fi and satellite television, ensuring guests can stay connected if desired.

270.

Sourdough Lodge embraces the spirit of community, often organizing social gatherings and activities where guests can interact and share their experiences.

271.

The lodge offers seasonal packages and special deals, making it accessible to a wide range of travelers with different budgets.

272.

Sourdough Lodge has a rich culinary tradition, serving homemade meals prepared with locally sourced ingredients and traditional recipes.

273.

The lodge's staff members are knowledgeable about the local area and can provide recommendations for nearby attractions and points of interest.

274.

Sourdough Lodge is located in an area with low light pollution, making it an excellent spot for stargazing and observing the night sky.

275.

The lodge has a dedicated team of outdoor guides and experts who can assist guests in planning and executing their wilderness adventures.

276.

Sourdough Lodge has a strong commitment to customer satisfaction, continuously striving to exceed guests' expectations and create memorable experiences.

277.

The lodge is open year-round, offering different activities and experiences depending on the season, from skiing and snowshoeing in winter to hiking and wildlife observation in summer.

278.

Sourdough Lodge supports local artisans and craftsmen, showcasing their work through displays and offering unique handmade souvenirs for purchase.

279.

The lodge's restaurant features a menu that highlights regional specialties, allowing guests to savor the flavors of the area.

280.

Sourdough Lodge has a cozy fireplace where guests can gather and relax after a day of outdoor exploration.

281.

The lodge is situated in a designated wilderness area, ensuring the preservation of the natural environment and wildlife habitat.

282.

Sourdough Lodge hosts workshops and educational programs that promote environmental awareness and conservation among guests.

283.

The lodge provides transportation services to nearby attractions and recreational areas, facilitating convenient access for guests.

284.

Sourdough Lodge has partnerships with local adventure outfitters, offering guests the opportunity to participate in thrilling activities such as river rafting and zip-lining.

285.

The lodge's surroundings are teeming with wildlife, including bears, moose, eagles, and various species of fish, providing endless opportunities for wildlife enthusiasts.

286.

Sourdough Lodge is known for its delicious homemade baked goods, with freshly baked bread, pastries, and desserts available for guests to enjoy.

287.

The lodge has a communal kitchen area where guests can prepare their meals, fostering a sense of community and shared experiences.

288.

Sourdough Lodge supports sustainable tourism practices, promoting responsible travel and encouraging guests to minimize their impact on the environment.

289.

The lodge offers a range of wellness activities, including yoga classes, massage services, and outdoor meditation areas, allowing guests to unwind and rejuvenate.

290.

Sourdough Lodge collaborates with local cultural organizations to provide guests with opportunities to learn about the region's indigenous cultures and traditions.

291.

The lodge's location provides access to pristine rivers and lakes, offering excellent fishing opportunities for anglers of all levels.

292.

Sourdough Lodge organizes photography workshops led by professional photographers, helping guests capture stunning images of the surrounding landscapes and wildlife.

293.

The lodge's staff members are passionate outdoor enthusiasts themselves, eager to share their knowledge and expertise with guests.

294.

Sourdough Lodge offers customized adventure packages, allowing guests to tailor their experience based on their preferences and interests.

295.

The lodge has a comfortable library area where guests can relax, read books, and learn about the history and ecology of the area.

296.

Sourdough Lodge supports local conservation initiatives, contributing to projects that aim to protect and restore the region's natural habitats.

297.

The lodge's location provides opportunities for cross-country skiing and snowmobiling during the winter months, attracting winter sports enthusiasts.

298.

Sourdough Lodge has a beautiful garden area where guests can unwind, surrounded by vibrant flowers, aromatic herbs, and tranquil seating areas.

299.

The lodge offers educational programs for children, introducing them to the wonders of nature and fostering a sense of environmental stewardship.

300.

Sourdough Lodge is committed to preserving the wilderness experience for future generations, working towards sustainable practices and advocating for the protection of natural areas.

301.

Francis Lewis was born on March 21, 1713, in Llandaff, Wales.

302.

He immigrated to the British colonies in North America at the age of 21 and settled in New York.

303.

Lewis became a successful merchant, engaging in various business ventures including trading, shipping, and real estate.

304.

He established a successful trading partnership with his wife's family, the Ludlams, which greatly contributed to his wealth.

305.

Lewis served as a delegate from New York in the Continental Congress from 1775 to 1779.

306.

He signed the Declaration of Independence in 1776, representing New York alongside other notable Founding Fathers.

307.

Lewis was one of the wealthiest members of the Continental Congress and used his personal funds to support the American Revolutionary War.

308.

He faced personal hardship during the war as his home and property were confiscated by the British.

309.

Lewis's wife, Elizabeth Annesley Lewis, was captured by the British and imprisoned for several months during the war.

310.

After the war, Lewis served as a member of the New York State Assembly from 1784 to 1788.

311.

He played a crucial role in the ratification of the United States Constitution in New York.

312.

Lewis was known for his strong support of the Federalist Party and advocated for a strong central government.

313.

He was appointed as a commissioner to negotiate a treaty with the Creek and Cherokee Native American tribes in 1785.

314.

Lewis was known for his philanthropic endeavors and donated a significant portion of his wealth to charitable causes.

315.

He helped establish the Society for the Relief of Poor Widows with Small Children, which provided support to widows and orphans.

316.

Lewis was an advocate for education and donated funds to establish the first public school in Whitestone, Queens.

317.

He owned extensive land holdings, including several large estates in New York and Long Island.

318.

Lewis's estate in Whitestone, known as the Francis Lewis Estate, is now a designated historic site and museum.

319.

He was an avid supporter of religious freedom and played a role in the establishment of St. George's Episcopal Church in Flushing, New York.

320.

Lewis was respected for his integrity and honesty in his business dealings, earning him a reputation as a trustworthy merchant.

321.

He was fluent in multiple languages, including English, Latin, Greek, French, and Dutch.

322.

Lewis's signature on the Declaration of Independence is one of the most recognizable and distinctive among the signatories.

323.

He served as a member of the New York Constitutional Convention in 1788, where he advocated for the ratification of the Constitution.

324.

Lewis retired from public life in 1789 but continued to be involved in philanthropic activities.

325.

He experienced financial difficulties in his later years and relied on the support of friends and family.

326.

Lewis passed away on December 31, 1803, at the age of 90 in New York City.

327.

He is buried in the Trinity Church Cemetery in Manhattan, where a memorial plaque commemorates his contributions to American independence.

328.

Lewis's legacy lives on through the many institutions and places named in his honor, including Francis Lewis High School in Queens, New York.

329.

He was known for his resilience and determination, as he persevered through personal losses and hardships during the Revolutionary War.

330.

Lewis's advocacy for a strong central government and his commitment to the ideals of the American Revolution shaped the early years of the United States.

331.

He was known for his eloquence and persuasive speaking abilities, often using his influence to garner support for important causes.

332.

Lewis's personal letters and correspondence provide valuable insights into the events and challenges faced during the Revolutionary War era.

333.

He was an active participant in the political and social life of New York, attending numerous meetings and gatherings related to the cause of independence.

334.

Lewis's role as a signer of the Declaration of Independence solidified his place in American history as one of the nation's founding fathers.

335.

He was a strong advocate for trade and commerce, recognizing the importance of economic prosperity in building a successful nation.

336.

Lewis's commitment to religious freedom and tolerance reflected the principles of the Enlightenment era and the values of the new nation.

337.

He was known for his love of learning and intellectual pursuits, regularly engaging in philosophical and political discussions with his peers.

338.

Lewis was a dedicated family man, raising seven children with his wife Elizabeth, whom he married in 1745.

339.

He had a close friendship with fellow Founding Father John Adams and corresponded with him on various political and personal matters.

340.

Lewis's dedication to public service and the cause of independence earned him the respect and admiration of his peers.

341.

He played a significant role in the formation of the new government of the United States, contributing to the establishment of the federal system.

342.

Lewis's contributions to the American Revolution were not limited to his financial support but also included his involvement in diplomatic efforts and negotiations.

343.

He was known for his strong moral character and ethical principles, which guided his actions and decisions throughout his life.

344.

Lewis's business acumen and entrepreneurial spirit contributed to the economic growth and development of New York during the colonial and post-revolutionary periods.

345.

He was a proponent of agricultural advancements and experimented with new farming techniques on his estates.

346.

Lewis's commitment to liberty and justice extended beyond his own interests, as he actively supported the abolitionist movement and worked to end slavery.

347.

He was instrumental in the establishment of the New York Chamber of Commerce, an organization that promoted trade and economic development in the state.

348.

Lewis's support for the arts and culture was evident in his patronage of artists and writers, fostering creativity and intellectual growth in the community.

349.

He was a dedicated patriot, willing to sacrifice his personal wealth and comfort for the cause of American independence.

350.

Lewis's contributions to the early years of the United States, both as a signer of the Declaration of Independence and as a respected statesman, solidified his place in American history as a key figure in the nation's founding.

351.

Philip Livingston was born on January 15, 1716, in Albany, New York.

352.

He came from a wealthy and influential family, known for their involvement in politics and business.

353.

Livingston attended Yale College, where he received a classical education.

354.

He joined his family's merchant business and became a successful
trader and landowner.

355.

Livingston was elected to the New York Provincial Assembly in
1759 and served as a representative for many years.

356.

He was an early advocate for colonial independence and actively
supported the cause of American liberty.

357.

Livingston was one of the signers of the Declaration of
Independence, representing the state of New York.

358.

He signed the document with a bold and distinctive signature,
making it easily recognizable.

359.

Livingston played a significant role in New York politics during the
Revolutionary War, serving on various committees and councils.

360.

He was elected to the Continental Congress and served from 1775
until his death in 1778.

361.

Livingston was known for his eloquence and persuasive speaking
abilities, often using his influence to rally support for the American
cause.

362.

He was a member of the Committee of Five, responsible for drafting the Declaration of Independence.

363.

Livingston supported the idea of a strong central government and was involved in the drafting of the Articles of Confederation.

364.

He advocated for the abolition of slavery and was an early supporter of emancipation efforts in New York.

365.

Livingston was a philanthropist and donated a significant portion of his wealth to charitable causes.

366.

He was a patron of the arts and supported the development of cultural institutions in New York.

367.

Livingston was one of the founders of Kings College, now known as Columbia University, and served on its Board of Governors.

368.

He played a crucial role in the establishment of the New York Manumission Society, an organization dedicated to the abolition of slavery.

369.

Livingston's commitment to religious freedom led him to support the establishment of the first Jewish synagogue in New York City.

370.

He was a member of the New York Committee of Safety, which oversaw the defense of the colony during the Revolutionary War.

371.

Livingston's personal finances suffered during the war, as he faced financial losses due to British occupation and confiscated property.

372.

He was known for his integrity and honesty in his business dealings, earning him a reputation as a trusted merchant.

373.

Livingston was an active member of the Masonic fraternity and held leadership positions within the organization.

374.

He married Christina Ten Broeck in 1740, and they had nine children together.

375.

Livingston's son, Henry Brockholst Livingston, later became a Justice of the United States Supreme Court.

376.

He was a member of the New York Committee of Correspondence, which facilitated communication between the colonies during the pre-revolutionary period.

377.

Livingston's health began to deteriorate in the late 1770s, and he passed away on June 12, 1778, at the age of 62.

378.

He is buried in the family vault at the Livingston Family Cemetery in Clermont, New York.

379.

Livingston's contributions to the cause of independence were recognized and honored by his contemporaries and future generations.

380.

His home, Clermont Manor, is now a designated National Historic Landmark and is open to the public as a museum.

381.

Livingston's legacy as a Founding Father and signatory of the Declaration of Independence remains an important part of American history.

382.

He was known for his meticulous record-keeping and left behind extensive correspondence and documents that provide valuable insights into the Revolutionary period.

383.

Livingston's dedication to public service and his unwavering commitment to the principles of liberty continue to inspire generations of Americans.

384.

He was a respected statesman and leader who played a crucial role in shaping the early years of the United States.

385.

Livingston's influence extended beyond his political career, as he was an active supporter of educational institutions and cultural development.

386.

He was known for his diplomatic skills and negotiation abilities, which were essential during the challenging times of the Revolutionary War.

387.

Livingston's strong character and principled stance on issues earned him the trust and respect of his peers.

388.

He was a firm believer in the power of education and promoted the establishment of schools and libraries in New York.

389.

Livingston's wealth and resources allowed him to support the Continental Army financially, contributing to the war effort.

390.

He was a staunch defender of individual rights and personal freedoms, advocating for the protection of civil liberties.

391.

Livingston's dedication to the cause of independence often put him at odds with loyalists and British sympathizers in New York.

392.

He served as a delegate to the New York Provincial Congress and the New York State Senate.

393.

Livingston's influence extended beyond the realm of politics, as he actively supported scientific and technological advancements.

394.

He was an early proponent of agricultural improvements and encouraged farmers to adopt new techniques and practices.

395.

Livingston's commitment to religious tolerance and freedom of worship was reflected in his support for various religious denominations in New York.

396.

He was a member of the New York Society for the Promotion of Agriculture, an organization dedicated to advancing agricultural knowledge and practices.

397.

Livingston's contributions to the development of New York as a thriving commercial center were significant, as he played a key role in the expansion of trade and commerce.

398.

He was a visionary leader who recognized the potential of New York as an economic powerhouse and worked to harness its resources and opportunities.

399.

Livingston's personal library was extensive, reflecting his intellectual curiosity and love for learning.

400.

His dedication to the ideals of liberty, equality, and justice remains an enduring legacy that continues to inspire and guide generations of Americans.

401.

The Atlas beetle (Chalcosoma atlas) is one of the largest species of beetles in the world, with males reaching lengths of up to 11 centimeters (4.3 inches).

402.

They are native to Southeast Asia, including countries like Malaysia, Indonesia, and Thailand.

403.

Atlas beetles have a distinct black or dark brown exoskeleton that is glossy and smooth.

404.

Males of the species are known for their impressive curved horns, which can be up to twice the length of their bodies. These horns are used in territorial battles with other males.

405.

Female Atlas beetles do not have horns and are generally smaller in size compared to males.

406.

The larvae of Atlas beetles are large and resemble wood grubs. They live in rotting logs and feed on decaying wood.

407.

Atlas beetles are primarily nocturnal creatures and are most active during the night.

408.

They are strong fliers and can be seen flying around forested areas in search of mates and food.

409.

The diet of Atlas beetles consists mainly of fruit sap, nectar, and tree sap. They are also known to feed on fallen fruits and dung.

410.

The lifespan of Atlas beetles is relatively short, with adults living for only a few months.

411.

Male Atlas beetles engage in intense battles over territory and mating rights. These fights involve pushing and shoving, as well as locking horns, to assert dominance.

412.

The horns of male Atlas beetles are not used for fighting or defending against predators but rather for intraspecies competition.

413.

Atlas beetles have a strong exoskeleton that provides protection against predators such as birds, reptiles, and mammals.

414.

They are generally non-aggressive insects and prefer to retreat or play dead when threatened.

415.

The larvae of Atlas beetles undergo a series of molts before reaching their full size. Each molt results in the shedding of the old exoskeleton and the growth of a new one.

416.

Atlas beetles have a lifespan of approximately one to two years, including the larval stage.

417.

The size of Atlas beetles varies among individuals and is influenced by factors such as food availability and environmental conditions.

418.

Male Atlas beetles produce a unique pheromone to attract females for mating. The scent is released from glands located on the underside of their bodies.

419.

After mating, female Atlas beetles lay their eggs in decaying wood or other suitable materials for the larvae to feed on.

420.

The larvae of Atlas beetles can take several months to complete their development before pupating into adults.

421.

The exoskeleton of Atlas beetles is composed of a tough material called chitin, which provides structural support and protection.

422.

Atlas beetles have strong mandibles that they use to grip and manipulate food.

423.

They have a relatively slow reproductive rate compared to other insects.

424.

The flight of Atlas beetles is characterized by a loud buzzing sound produced by the rapid movement of their wings.

425.

Atlas beetles are attracted to bright lights and can often be found near street lamps and other illuminated areas at night.

426.

The population of Atlas beetles is threatened by habitat loss due to deforestation and urbanization.

427.

Conservation efforts are being made to protect the habitats of Atlas beetles and ensure their survival in the wild.

428.

Atlas beetles play an important role in the ecosystem as decomposers, aiding in the breakdown of decaying organic matter.

429.

They are sometimes kept as pets by insect enthusiasts and collectors.

430.

Atlas beetles have been featured in traditional folklore and myths in Southeast Asian cultures, often symbolizing strength and power.

431.

They are highly sought after by insect collectors due to their impressive size and unique appearance.

432.

The impressive horns of male Atlas beetles have been used in various forms of artwork and jewelry.

433.

Atlas beetles are known to have a strong grip and can cling onto surfaces with their legs.

434.

They are not considered pests and do not cause damage to crops or structures.

435.

The Atlas beetle belongs to the family Scarabaeidae, which includes other well-known beetles like the dung beetle and rhinoceros beetle.

436.

Their large size and unique appearance make them a popular subject for scientific research and study.

437.

Atlas beetles have specialized adaptations to their habitats, including the ability to camouflage themselves among leaves and tree bark.

438.

They have been successfully bred in captivity for educational purposes and conservation efforts.

439.

Atlas beetles are capable of producing sound by rubbing body parts together, which can serve as a warning to potential predators.

440.

The lifespan of Atlas beetles can vary depending on factors such as temperature, humidity, and food availability.

441.

The body of Atlas beetles is divided into three main sections: the head, thorax, and abdomen.

442.

They have compound eyes that provide them with a wide field of vision.

443.

Atlas beetles are not known to be aggressive towards humans and rarely bite or sting.

444.

The metallic sheen of their exoskeleton is caused by microscopic structures that reflect and scatter light.

445.

They are capable of lifting objects many times their own body weight with their powerful legs.

446.

Atlas beetles have a well-developed sense of smell, which helps them locate food sources and mates.

447.

The population of Atlas beetles in the wild is declining due to habitat destruction and illegal trade.

448.

They are generally solitary insects, only coming together for mating purposes.

449.

Atlas beetles have been featured in various forms of artwork, literature, and cultural expressions across different societies.

450.

Their ecological role as decomposers contributes to nutrient cycling and the overall health of forest ecosystems.

451.

Audubon's Shearwater (Puffinus lherminieri) is a species of seabird found in tropical and subtropical regions of the Atlantic Ocean.

452.

They are named after John James Audubon, a renowned ornithologist and naturalist.

453.

These birds are medium-sized, measuring around 30-35 centimeters (12-14 inches) in length.

454.

Audubon's Shearwaters have a dark brown or blackish upper body and a white underbelly.

455.

They have long, slender wings, which enable them to soar and glide effortlessly over the ocean.

456.

These birds are known for their graceful flight, often appearing as if they are dancing above the water.

457.

Audubon's Shearwaters are highly adapted to life at sea and are rarely seen on land, except during the breeding season.

458.

They have a wingspan of approximately 60-70 centimeters (24-28 inches).

459.

The diet of Audubon's Shearwaters mainly consists of fish and squid, which they catch by diving into the water from the air.

460.

They are capable of diving to depths of up to 30 meters (98 feet) in search of prey.

461.

Audubon's Shearwaters are known for their strong sense of smell, which helps them locate food sources.

462.

Breeding colonies of Audubon's Shearwaters are typically found on remote islands and rocky cliffs.

463.

They nest in burrows dug into the ground or under vegetation, providing protection for their eggs and chicks.

464.

The breeding season for Audubon's Shearwaters typically occurs between April and September.

465.

Both males and females take turns incubating the single egg and caring for the chick.

466.

The chicks are initially covered in down feathers and are fed regurgitated food by their parents.

467.

Audubon's Shearwaters are known for their distinctive calls, which include a variety of whistles, screeches, and croaks.

468.

They are highly social birds and often gather in large flocks when foraging or resting on the water's surface.

469.

Audubon's Shearwaters are excellent swimmers, using their webbed feet to propel themselves through the water.

470.

They have a lifespan of around 15-25 years in the wild.

471.

Audubon's Shearwaters are migratory birds, traveling long distances between breeding and non-breeding grounds.

472.

During migration, they can cover thousands of kilometers, relying on their exceptional navigation skills.

473.

These birds are known to undertake nocturnal migrations, using the stars and Earth's magnetic field as guides.

474.

Audubon's Shearwaters are susceptible to threats such as pollution, habitat destruction, and entanglement in fishing gear.

475.

Conservation efforts are underway to protect their breeding sites and ensure the sustainability of their populations.

476.

They are classified as a species of least concern by the International Union for Conservation of Nature (IUCN).

477.

Audubon's Shearwaters play a role in the marine ecosystem by transferring nutrients between different areas through their feeding activities.

478.

These birds have been the subject of scientific research to understand their behavior, migration patterns, and population dynamics.

479.

Audubon's Shearwaters are sometimes affected by oil spills, which can harm their plumage and disrupt their foraging abilities.

480.

They have a streamlined body shape, which reduces drag and allows them to fly efficiently.

481.

The feathers of Audubon's Shearwaters are waterproof, enabling them to remain buoyant and dry while diving.

482.

They are part of the Procellariidae family, which includes other shearwaters, petrels, and albatrosses.

483.

Audubon's Shearwaters are known to exhibit strong site fidelity, returning to the same breeding grounds year after year.

484.

They have sharp beaks that help them catch and consume their prey.

485.

Audubon's Shearwaters are often seen in association with other seabirds, such as gulls and terns.

486.

They are capable of flying long distances without flapping their wings, taking advantage of air currents and updrafts.

487.

Audubon's Shearwaters have a unique odor, which has been described as a combination of fishy and earthy scents.

488.

They have a gland near the base of their tail that produces an oil used for preening and waterproofing their feathers.

489.

These birds are known to be monogamous, forming long-term pair bonds with their mates.

490.

Audubon's Shearwaters have a strong instinct for returning to their natal colonies to breed, even after years spent at sea.

491.

They are sometimes referred to as tropical shearwaters or tropical petrels.

492.

Audubon's Shearwaters are capable of flying at high speeds, reaching up to 55 kilometers per hour (34 miles per hour).

493.

They have adapted to flying in low-light conditions, with specialized retinas in their eyes that enhance their night vision.

494.

These birds have a glandular stomach that produces an oily substance used to feed their chicks.

495.

Audubon's Shearwaters are known to engage in courtship displays, including aerial acrobatics and vocalizations.

496.

They have a relatively low reproductive rate, with females typically laying only one egg per breeding season.

497.

Audubon's Shearwaters are known to return to the same nesting burrow year after year, often using the same mate.

498.

These birds have been observed following fishing vessels to scavenge on discarded fish and offal.

499.

Audubon's Shearwaters are sensitive to disturbances at their breeding sites and may abandon their nests if disturbed.

500.

They are a beloved species among birdwatchers and nature enthusiasts, who appreciate their grace, beauty, and importance in marine ecosystems.

501.

The 1956 Grand Canyon TWA-United Airlines aviation accident occurred on June 30, 1956.

502.

It was a mid-air collision between a Trans World Airlines (TWA) Lockheed L-1049 Super Constellation and a United Airlines Douglas DC-7.

503.

The collision happened over the Grand Canyon in Arizona, resulting in the loss of both aircraft and the deaths of all 128 passengers and crew members on board.

504.

The accident was one of the deadliest in aviation history at the time and led to significant changes in air traffic control and aviation safety regulations.

505.

The TWA flight, known as Flight 2, was en route from Los Angeles to Kansas City with a scheduled stop in Chicago.

506.

The United Airlines flight, known as Flight 718, was traveling from Los Angeles to Chicago.

507.

The collision occurred due to a combination of factors, including poor visibility, limited radar coverage, and the absence of collision avoidance systems.

508.

The crash site spans an area of approximately 1.5 square miles within the Grand Canyon National Park.

509.

The debris from the two aircraft was scattered across the rugged and remote terrain of the canyon, making recovery and investigation efforts challenging.

510.

The wreckage of the aircraft and the remains of the victims were initially discovered by a United States Marine Corps helicopter pilot who was conducting a routine flight in the area.

511.

The accident prompted a comprehensive investigation by the Civil Aeronautics Board (CAB), which focused on improving air traffic control procedures and increasing the use of radar for aircraft separation.

512.

The investigation led to the implementation of stricter regulations for flight planning, routing, and communication between air traffic control and pilots.

513.

The accident also highlighted the need for improved crash survivability features in aircraft, such as strengthened cabin structures and fire-resistant materials.

514.

The crash site is considered a memorial to the victims, and a bronze plaque was placed at the location to honor their memory.

515.

Access to the crash site is restricted to preserve the integrity of the area and out of respect for the victims and their families.

<h1 style="text-align:center">516.</h1>

The accident had a profound impact on the aviation industry and led to significant advancements in air safety, including the development of collision avoidance systems and the establishment of the Federal Aviation Administration (FAA) in 1958.

<h1 style="text-align:center">517.</h1>

The investigation into the accident was one of the most extensive and thorough in aviation history, involving experts from various fields and agencies.

<h1 style="text-align:center">518.</h1>

The collision occurred at an altitude of approximately 21,000 feet (6,400 meters) above sea level.

<h1 style="text-align:center">519.</h1>

It is believed that the collision happened within seconds of the two aircraft entering the same airspace due to a combination of navigation errors and miscommunications.

<h1 style="text-align:center">520.</h1>

The crash resulted in widespread public attention and highlighted the need for improved air traffic control infrastructure and procedures.

<h1 style="text-align:center">521.</h1>

The accident was a catalyst for the development and implementation of the modern air traffic control system that relies on radar, radio communication, and standardized procedures.

<h1 style="text-align:center">522.</h1>

The Grand Canyon crash was a pivotal moment in aviation history and served as a stark reminder of the importance of safety in air travel.

523.

The accident also had a significant impact on the families of the victims, who experienced immense grief and loss.

524.

The tragedy prompted calls for improved training and oversight of air traffic controllers to ensure the highest level of safety in the skies.

525.

The crash site is considered a solemn reminder of the lives lost and a symbol of the ongoing efforts to enhance aviation safety.

526.

The National Park Service manages and protects the crash site as part of the Grand Canyon National Park, ensuring its preservation for future generations.

527.

The accident led to advancements in aircraft collision avoidance technologies, including the development of the Traffic Collision Avoidance System (TCAS) that is widely used in commercial aviation today.

528.

The investigation into the accident was one of the first to use flight data recorders and cockpit voice recorders extensively, providing valuable insights into the sequence of events leading to the collision.

529.

The crash resulted in an increased focus on pilot training and the importance of crew resource management to improve communication and decision-making in the cockpit.

530.

The accident prompted changes in airspace design and routing to minimize the risk of mid-air collisions, including the establishment of designated airways and altitude separation requirements.

531.

The tragedy also spurred advancements in aircraft emergency locator transmitters (ELTs) to aid in locating and recovering downed aircraft.

532.

The crash site serves as a reminder of the human cost of aviation accidents and the ongoing efforts to prevent such tragedies through enhanced safety measures and technological advancements.

533.

The accident had a lasting impact on the families of the victims, who fought for improved aviation safety regulations and continued to honor the memory of their loved ones.

534.

The crash site remains a place of remembrance and reflection, visited by those seeking to pay their respects to the victims and learn from the lessons of the accident.

535.

The accident highlighted the need for improved coordination and communication between different airlines and air traffic control centers to ensure the safe operation of flights.

536.

The crash site is marked with a memorial plaque and serves as a place for quiet contemplation and remembrance of the lives lost.

537.

The tragedy led to advancements in aircraft crash investigations, including the establishment of standardized protocols for evidence collection and analysis.

538.

The accident prompted the development of emergency response protocols for air crashes, ensuring a coordinated and efficient approach to rescue and recovery efforts.

539.

The crash site is a testament to the resilience of the human spirit and the strength of communities coming together in times of tragedy.

540.

The accident served as a catalyst for international collaboration and the sharing of best practices in aviation safety to prevent similar incidents in the future.

541.

The crash site is a designated historical landmark, preserving the memory of the accident and its impact on aviation history.

542.

The tragedy prompted changes in air traffic control training programs, emphasizing the importance of situational awareness and clear communication.

543.

The accident served as a wake-up call for the aviation industry, leading to renewed efforts to enhance safety protocols and reduce the risk of mid-air collisions.

544.

The crash site serves as a reminder of the ongoing commitment to improve aviation safety and prevent accidents through continuous learning and innovation.

545.

The tragedy highlighted the importance of effective leadership and decision-making in aviation operations, sparking discussions on crew coordination and resource management.

546.

The accident led to the development of comprehensive accident investigation procedures, ensuring that all relevant factors are considered in determining the cause of an aviation accident.

547.

The crash site attracts aviation enthusiasts and historians who are interested in understanding the circumstances surrounding the accident and its impact on aviation safety.

548.

The tragedy led to advancements in aircraft tracking technologies, including the implementation of radar-based surveillance systems to enhance the monitoring of aircraft in flight.

549.

The crash site is a place of reverence and reflection, reminding visitors of the fragility of human life and the importance of prioritizing safety in aviation.

550.

The accident sparked conversations on the ethical responsibilities of the aviation industry, leading to a renewed commitment to passenger safety and well-being.

551.

Air Force Facility Missile Site 8, also known as AFM-8, was a missile launch site located in South Dakota, United States.

552.

It was an underground facility designed to launch Minuteman Intercontinental Ballistic Missiles (ICBMs) during the Cold War era.

553.

AFM-8 was one of the many missile sites established as part of the United States' nuclear deterrence strategy.

554.

The facility was active from the 1960s until its decommissioning in the 1990s.

555.

It was part of the 44th Missile Wing, which was responsible for maintaining and operating the Minuteman ICBMs.

556.

The missile site consisted of an underground launch control center (LCC) and an underground missile silo.

557.

The LCC housed the missile launch control officers and the equipment necessary to monitor and control the missile.

558.

The missile silo contained the Minuteman ICBM, which was capable of delivering a nuclear warhead to targets thousands of miles away.

559.

The site was heavily fortified and designed to withstand various threats, including nuclear attacks.

560.

The launch of the Minuteman ICBMs from AFM-8 would have been a retaliatory measure in the event of a nuclear conflict.

561.

The site was kept on high alert, with 24/7 staffing to ensure readiness to launch the missiles if necessary.

562.

AFM-8 played a critical role in the United States' nuclear deterrence strategy during the Cold War, serving as a deterrent against potential adversaries.

563.

The facility was equipped with advanced communication systems to maintain constant contact with higher command authorities.

564.

Security measures at the site were strict, with limited access and stringent protocols to prevent unauthorized entry.

565.

The personnel assigned to AFM-8 underwent rigorous training to ensure they could operate the missile system effectively and respond appropriately to any contingencies.

566.

The missiles housed at the site were regularly inspected, tested, and maintained to ensure their operational readiness.

567.

The construction of AFM-8 required extensive excavation and reinforced concrete structures to provide protection against enemy attacks.

568.

The missile launch process involved a series of intricate steps, including pre-launch checks, target selection, and coordination with other missile sites.

569.

AFM-8 was part of a larger network of missile sites strategically positioned across the United States, ensuring comprehensive coverage and redundancy.

570.

The facility operated under strict protocols and strict adherence to the principles of nuclear safety and arms control agreements.

571.

AFM-8 represented a significant investment of resources and technology by the United States government to maintain a credible nuclear deterrent.

572.

The facility was staffed by a highly trained and dedicated team of military personnel responsible for its operation and maintenance.

573.

AFM-8 had a sophisticated security system that included surveillance cameras, perimeter fencing, and armed guards to protect the site.

574.

The missile launch sequence involved multiple layers of authorization and verification to prevent accidental or unauthorized launches.

575.

The site's location was chosen strategically to maximize the effectiveness of the missile's range and minimize the risk of collateral damage.

576.

AFM-8 served as a symbol of the United States' commitment to nuclear deterrence and its preparedness to defend against potential threats.

577.

The facility's existence was highly classified, and its precise location was known only to authorized personnel.

578.

The missiles stored at AFM-8 were fueled and ready to launch within minutes of receiving the order.

579.

The facility was designed with redundant systems and backup power sources to ensure its operational continuity in case of emergencies.

580.

AFM-8 underwent periodic inspections by higher command authorities to assess its readiness and compliance with security protocols.

581.

The facility maintained a close relationship with nearby support units, such as maintenance and security forces, to ensure its smooth operation.

582.

AFM-8 represented a significant technological achievement, with the Minuteman ICBM being one of the most advanced missile systems of its time.

583.

The site had provisions for long-term sustainability, including food, water, and medical supplies, to support the personnel in the event of extended periods of isolation.

584.

The launch control officers assigned to AFM-8 underwent intensive training and were subject to strict security clearances due to the sensitive nature of their responsibilities.

585.

The missiles housed at the site were periodically replaced and upgraded to incorporate technological advancements and ensure their effectiveness as a deterrent.

586.

The facility's personnel were prepared to operate under high-stress conditions, knowing that their actions could have significant consequences in times of crisis.

587.

AFM-8 remained operational throughout the Cold War, with its mission evolving as the geopolitical landscape shifted.

588.

The site's closure and decommissioning were part of the arms control agreements and reductions between the United States and Russia.

589.

Today, the remnants of AFM-8 serve as a reminder of the Cold War era and the global tensions that shaped military strategies and technologies.

590.

The facility's decommissioning process involved the removal of the missiles, deactivation of launch systems, and securing the site against unauthorized access.

591.

The site's location is now classified as a former military installation, and access is restricted to authorized personnel only.

592.

AFM-8 played a critical role in maintaining the delicate balance of power during the Cold War, ensuring deterrence and avoiding the escalation of conflicts.

593.

The facility's operations were shrouded in secrecy, and its existence was known only to a select few within the military and government.

594.

The personnel assigned to AFM-8 lived in close-knit communities and developed strong bonds, relying on each other for support during their time on duty.

595.

The missiles housed at the site were regularly inspected and maintained to ensure their reliability and readiness to perform their intended function.

596.

AFM-8's closure marked the end of an era in nuclear deterrence, as the focus shifted towards arms control agreements and nonproliferation efforts.

597.

The site's decommissioning process followed strict protocols to ensure the proper disposal of hazardous materials and the restoration of the environment.

598.

AFM-8's operational readiness was constantly assessed through drills, simulations, and exercises to ensure the effectiveness of its response capabilities.

599.

The facility's existence and mission were not publicly acknowledged until several years after its decommissioning, highlighting the level of secrecy surrounding its operations.

600.

AFM-8 serves as a testament to the dedication and sacrifices of the military personnel who served there, contributing to the country's defense and security during a tense period in history.

601.

James Logan was born on October 20, 1674, in Ireland and later immigrated to the American colonies.

602.

He played a crucial role in the founding of the Pennsylvania Colony and became one of its most influential figures.

603.

Logan served as the secretary to William Penn, the founder of Pennsylvania, and developed a close relationship with him.

604.

He was highly educated and had a keen interest in science, literature, and philosophy.

605.

Logan was proficient in several languages, including Latin, Greek, Hebrew, and French.

606.

He played a key role in negotiating treaties with Native American tribes, helping to establish peaceful relations between the settlers and the indigenous people.

607.

Logan was appointed as the chief justice of the Pennsylvania Supreme Court in 1731 and served in that role for over 20 years.

608.

He was known for his impartiality and fairness in making legal decisions, earning him a reputation as a respected jurist.

609.

Logan was a prominent advocate for freedom of speech and press, believing in the importance of open dialogue and the exchange of ideas.

610.

He had a vast personal library, which became the foundation for the creation of the Library Company of Philadelphia, one of America's first public libraries.

611.

Logan corresponded with many influential intellectuals of his time, including Benjamin Franklin and Isaac Newton.

612.

He played a significant role in the founding of the University of Pennsylvania, serving as one of its earliest trustees.

613.

Logan's interest in botany led him to cultivate one of the most extensive private gardens in colonial America, featuring a wide variety of plants from around the world.

614.

He made significant contributions to the field of natural history and botany, documenting and collecting specimens from the American wilderness.

615.

Logan was a staunch supporter of religious tolerance, promoting the idea of freedom of worship and respecting the rights of different religious communities.

616.

He served as the mayor of Philadelphia in 1722 and worked to improve the city's infrastructure and public services.

617.

Logan's home, Stenton, located in Philadelphia, is now a historic site and museum, preserving his legacy and showcasing colonial-era architecture.

618.

He had a strong interest in Native American culture and was known for his collection of Native American artifacts, which he displayed in his home.

619.

Logan was involved in the political affairs of the colony, advocating for representative government and fair treatment of all citizens.

620.

He was a proponent of public education and believed in the importance of accessible education for all, regardless of social or economic status.

621.

Logan's contributions to science and botany were recognized by the Linnean Society of London, which elected him as a member in 1741.

622.

He was a philanthropist and actively supported various charitable causes, including orphanages and hospitals.

623.

Logan's efforts in promoting peace and diplomacy with Native American tribes helped to prevent conflicts and fostered cooperation between different cultures.

624.

He played a key role in establishing the Pennsylvania Gazette, one of the earliest and most influential newspapers in the American colonies.

625.

Logan's diplomatic skills and negotiation abilities were crucial in resolving boundary disputes between Pennsylvania and neighboring colonies.

626.

He was deeply committed to public service and dedicated his life to
the betterment of the Pennsylvania Colony.

627.

Logan was an influential figure in the early development of
Philadelphia as a cultural and intellectual center.

628.

He advocated for fair trade practices and worked to establish
economic policies that would benefit both the colonists and the
indigenous peoples.

629.

Logan's writings and correspondences provide valuable insights into
the political, social, and cultural climate of colonial America.

630.

He maintained a close friendship with William Penn's family, even
after Penn's death, and played a significant role in managing his
estate and preserving his legacy.

631.

Logan's commitment to justice and equality earned him the
admiration and respect of his peers and the people of Pennsylvania.

632.

He had a strong belief in the power of reason and rational thinking,
which guided his decision-making process and influenced his
philosophical views.

633.

Logan's advocacy for Native American rights and his efforts to
promote understanding and cooperation set an example for future
generations.

634.

He was known for his meticulous record-keeping and maintained detailed journals and diaries, providing valuable historical insights.

635.

Logan's leadership and administrative skills were crucial in the early development and success of the Pennsylvania Colony.

636.

He actively participated in the political debates of his time, advocating for the rights and liberties of the colonists.

637.

Logan's contributions to science and botany laid the foundation for future explorations and discoveries in the natural world.

638.

He was a strong supporter of public health initiatives and worked to improve sanitation and hygiene in Philadelphia.

639.

Logan's legacy continues to be celebrated in Pennsylvania, with numerous landmarks, institutions, and streets named in his honor.

640.

He was a member of the Free Society of Traders, a trading company that played a significant role in the economic development of the colony.

641.

Logan's commitment to public service and his tireless efforts to promote the welfare of the Pennsylvania Colony earned him widespread admiration.

642.

He played a pivotal role in the peaceful transition of power in Pennsylvania during the 1730s and 1740s.

643.

Logan's extensive network of contacts and relationships allowed him to navigate complex political landscapes and advance his causes effectively.

644.

He was a dedicated supporter of the Enlightenment ideals and believed in the power of education and knowledge to transform society.

645.

Logan's contributions to botany and natural history laid the groundwork for future scientific exploration and understanding of the American landscape.

646.

He was known for his eloquence and persuasive speaking abilities, making him a formidable figure in political and intellectual circles.

647.

Logan's commitment to religious tolerance and his belief in the separation of church and state influenced the development of religious freedom in the United States.

648.

He actively promoted the arts and culture, supporting initiatives that fostered creativity and intellectual growth in the colony.

649.

Logan's leadership and diplomatic skills were crucial in maintaining peaceful relations with neighboring colonies and tribes.

650.

He left a lasting legacy as a statesman, scholar, and advocate for justice, leaving a significant impact on the early history of Pennsylvania and the American colonies.

651.

Thomas Lynch Jr. was born on August 5, 1749, in South Carolina, to a prominent planter family.

652.

He was educated in England and attended Eton College and then Cambridge University.

653.

Lynch's father, Thomas Lynch Sr., was a signer of the Declaration of Independence, and his family was actively involved in politics.

654.

Lynch Jr. became a lawyer and practiced law in South Carolina before entering politics.

655.

At the age of 26, Lynch was elected to the Continental Congress in 1776 and served alongside other Founding Fathers.

656.

He was one of the youngest signers of the Declaration of Independence, signing it on August 2, 1776.

657.

Lynch's signature on the Declaration of Independence is known for its elegant and distinct penmanship.

658.

He was a strong advocate for independence and played a significant role in rallying support for the Revolutionary cause.

659.

Lynch was known for his eloquence and persuasive speaking skills, making him a respected orator and public figure.

660.

During his time in Congress, Lynch served on various committees, including the Committee of Safety and the Board of War.

661.

He was a vocal critic of British policies and actively supported the American Revolution, advocating for the rights and liberties of the colonists.

662.

In 1779, Lynch's health began to deteriorate, and he decided to travel to Europe for medical treatment.

663.

Unfortunately, Lynch's ship, the brigantine "Savannah," was lost at sea, and he, along with his wife and child, perished in the tragedy.

664.

The exact circumstances surrounding the loss of the "Savannah" remain a mystery, as no wreckage or survivors were ever found.

665.

Lynch's untimely death at the age of 30 cut short what could have been a promising political career.

666.

Despite his short life, Lynch's contributions to the American Revolution and the cause of independence were significant.

667.

He was a staunch supporter of individual liberty and believed in the importance of representative government.

668.

Lynch's dedication to the principles of freedom and justice continue to inspire generations of Americans.

669.

He was posthumously honored for his sacrifice and commitment to the American cause, with several monuments and memorials erected in his memory.

670.

Lynch's family estate, known as Hopsewee Plantation, still stands today and is listed on the National Register of Historic Places.

671.

He left behind a legacy of patriotism and devotion to the ideals of liberty and equality.

672.

Lynch's story is a reminder of the sacrifices made by the Founding Fathers in their pursuit of American independence.

673.

His name is immortalized in history as one of the signers of the Declaration of Independence, forever connected to the birth of a nation.

674.

Lynch's writings and correspondence provide valuable insights into the political and social climate of the Revolutionary era.

675.

He is often celebrated for his courage and commitment to the principles of self-governance.

676.

Lynch's tragic death at sea added a layer of mystery and intrigue to his story, leaving historians and researchers fascinated by the circumstances surrounding his disappearance.

677.

Lynch's early education in England exposed him to Enlightenment ideas and philosophical thought, shaping his political beliefs.

678.

He was deeply influenced by the ideals of the American Revolution and the concept of individual rights and freedoms.

679.

Lynch's family played a significant role in South Carolina's political and economic landscape, and he inherited a legacy of public service.

680.

Despite his relatively short time in Congress, Lynch's contributions to the Continental Congress and the cause of independence were highly valued by his peers.

681.

Lynch's signature on the Declaration of Independence represents his commitment to the ideals of liberty and the pursuit of a new nation.

682.

He was deeply engaged in the political debates of his time, advocating for the rights and liberties of the American colonists.

683.

Lynch's early death deprived the nation of a potential leader and statesman, leaving behind a sense of what could have been.

684.

His tragic fate at sea became a symbol of the risks and sacrifices made by those who fought for American independence.

685.

Lynch's legacy extends beyond his political career, as he is remembered for his intellect, charm, and dedication to the American cause.

686.

The loss of Lynch and his family on the ill-fated voyage of the "Savannah" serves as a poignant reminder of the dangers faced by those involved in the struggle for independence.

687.

Lynch's contributions to the formation of a new nation continue to be celebrated and honored, reminding us of the courage and conviction of the Founding Fathers.

688.

His story highlights the personal sacrifices made by individuals and their families during the American Revolution.

689.

Lynch's presence in the Continental Congress helped to solidify support for independence and fostered a sense of unity among the colonies.

690.

The legacy of Thomas Lynch Jr. is intertwined with the larger narrative of the American Revolution, reminding us of the sacrifices and struggles that paved the way for the birth of a nation.

691.

Lynch's commitment to the principles of self-governance and individual liberty resonates with the values that continue to define the United States.

692.

His name is often mentioned alongside other prominent Founding Fathers, such as George Washington, Thomas Jefferson, and John Adams, highlighting his significance in shaping the nation's destiny.

693.

Lynch's contributions to the Continental Congress and his dedication to the cause of American independence played a vital role in the ultimate success of the Revolution.

694.

Despite his relatively brief political career, Lynch's influence and impact on the founding of the United States cannot be overstated.

695.

His untimely death transformed him into a symbol of sacrifice and devotion to the ideals of freedom and democracy.

696.

Lynch's commitment to public service and his belief in the power of representative government continue to inspire individuals entering the field of politics.

697.

He was part of a generation of leaders who risked their lives and fortunes to secure the liberties and rights we enjoy today.

698.

Lynch's contributions to the American Revolution helped lay the foundation for the democratic principles that govern the nation.

699.

His story is a testament to the courage and determination of those who fought for independence and shaped the course of American history.

700.

The memory of Thomas Lynch Jr. lives on as a reminder of the sacrifices made by the Founding Fathers and their enduring impact on the nation's development.

701.

The Australasian Grebe, scientific name Tachybaptus novaehollandiae, is a small waterbird found in Australia, New Zealand, and New Guinea.

702.

It is also known by other names such as Australian Grebe, Little Grebe, and Dabchick.

703.

The Australasian Grebe is the smallest grebe species in Australia, measuring about 25 to 27 centimeters in length.

704.

It has a distinctive appearance with a small, rounded body, short neck, and a pointed bill.

705.

The plumage of the Australasian Grebe is mainly brown, with a darker back and lighter underparts.

706.

During breeding season, the birds develop a striking black and chestnut-colored neck and head.

707.

They have lobed toes with flattened, broadened webs, which aid in swimming and diving.

708.

Australasian Grebes are excellent divers and can stay submerged for up to 30 seconds while searching for prey.

709.

Their diet consists primarily of small aquatic invertebrates, such as insects, crustaceans, and small fish.

710.

They have a unique feeding behavior known as "flutter-dipping," where they swim rapidly on the surface, creating ripples to attract prey.

711.

The breeding season for Australasian Grebes typically occurs from September to March.

712.

During courtship, the male and female engage in elaborate displays, including neck stretching, head shaking, and synchronized diving.

713.

They build floating nests made of plant materials, anchored to aquatic vegetation or floating debris.

714.

Both parents take turns incubating the eggs, which usually hatch after around three weeks.

715.

The chicks are initially covered in fluffy gray down and are capable of swimming shortly after hatching.

716.

Australasian Grebes are highly territorial during the breeding season and defend their nesting territories aggressively.

717.

They are mostly solitary birds but can be seen in small groups or pairs outside of the breeding season.

718.

The species is known for its elaborate courtship vocalizations, which consist of a series of whistles, trills, and chirps.

719.

They have a widespread distribution across Australia, inhabiting freshwater lakes, rivers, wetlands, and estuaries.

720.

Australasian Grebes are skilled at camouflage, often blending in with their surroundings by pressing their bodies low in the water.

721.

They are vulnerable to predation by larger birds, such as eagles, hawks, and cormorants.

722.

The lifespan of Australasian Grebes is estimated to be around 5 to 6 years in the wild.

723.

The birds are highly sensitive to changes in water quality and habitat degradation, making them good indicators of environmental health.

724.

They have a rapid breeding cycle and can produce multiple broods in a single breeding season.

725.

The species is not migratory, although some individuals may undertake short-distance movements in response to changing conditions.

726.

In urban areas, Australasian Grebes can be found in artificial water bodies such as ponds, reservoirs, and park lakes.

727.

They have a unique adaptation known as "wing-pumping," where they rapidly beat their wings while floating on the water, possibly to dry their feathers or regulate body temperature.

728.

Australasian Grebes are known for their agile and nimble swimming abilities, making them highly maneuverable in the water.

729.

They have a distinct courtship dance that involves synchronized head movements and beak dipping.

730.

The species is not considered globally threatened, but local populations may face threats from habitat loss, pollution, and predation by introduced species.

731.

Australasian Grebes have been known to build their nests on the floating leaves of water lilies or reeds, providing protection from land-based predators.

732.

They are highly adaptable and can colonize new habitats, even those created by human activities such as dam construction.

733.

The birds are monogamous and typically form long-term pair bonds with their mates.

734.

They have a high metabolic rate and need to consume a significant amount of food daily to sustain their energy levels.

735.

The Australasian Grebe has excellent underwater vision, allowing it to spot prey even in murky waters.

736.

They have a unique courtship display called the "weed dance," where the male presents the female with floating vegetation as a gift.

737.

The species is known for its ability to camouflage its nests by covering them with floating vegetation or building them among dense reeds.

738.

The Australasian Grebe has a wide repertoire of vocalizations, including trills, whistles, purring sounds, and soft grunts.

739.

They have a rapid wingbeat while in flight, which enables them to take off quickly from the water's surface.

740.

The birds are generally silent during the non-breeding season and rely on visual signals and body language for communication.

741.

Australasian Grebes have a highly efficient digestive system, allowing them to extract nutrients from their prey effectively.

742.

They have excellent diving skills and can plunge underwater to catch prey at depths of up to 5 meters.

743.

The species has a complex mating system, with multiple males often courting a single female simultaneously.

744.

Australasian Grebes are known to engage in "foot-flagging" behavior, where they rapidly raise and lower one or both of their feet as a territorial display.

745.

They are capable of flying short distances, but their flight is relatively low and rapid, with frequent wingbeats.

746.

The birds have a well-developed preen gland at the base of their tail, which produces an oil used for waterproofing their feathers.

747.

Australasian Grebes are highly sensitive to disturbances and will quickly dive underwater to escape perceived threats.

748.

They have excellent hearing and can detect sounds both above and below the water's surface.

749.

The species has a strong affinity for freshwater habitats but can occasionally be found in brackish or saltwater environments.

750.

Australasian Grebes are fascinating waterbirds that exhibit unique behaviors, impressive diving capabilities, and striking plumage, making them a delight to observe in their natural habitats.

751.

The Australian Dingo, Canis lupus dingo, is a wild dog native to Australia.

752.

Dingoes are believed to have arrived in Australia approximately 4,000 years ago, likely brought by Asian seafarers.

753.

They are considered one of the oldest dog breeds, with genetic studies suggesting they diverged from domestic dogs around 8,000 to 10,000 years ago.

754.

Australian Dingoes are medium-sized dogs, weighing between 13 to 20 kilograms (29 to 44 pounds).

755.

They have a lean and muscular body with a head resembling that of a domestic dog but with longer muzzles and erect ears.

756.

The fur of Dingoes can vary in color, including shades of yellow, sandy, or reddish-brown, with lighter underparts.

757.

Dingoes have adapted well to various environments in Australia, including deserts, grasslands, and forests.

758.

They are highly agile and can cover long distances in search of food and water.

759.

Dingoes have a strong sense of smell and excellent eyesight, enabling them to hunt efficiently.

760.

Their diet is diverse and includes small mammals, birds, reptiles, and even insects.

761.

Dingoes are skilled hunters and often work in packs to capture larger prey, such as kangaroos or feral pigs.

762.

They are known for their distinctive and haunting howl, which serves as a vocal communication method between individuals and packs.

763.

Dingoes are highly adaptable and can survive in harsh conditions with limited water and food resources.

764.

They are territorial animals and mark their territories with urine and feces to communicate ownership and boundaries.

765.

Dingoes are opportunistic feeders and will scavenge from human settlements or consume carrion when available.

766.

Unlike domestic dogs, Dingoes have a more elongated and flexible spine, allowing them to twist and turn while hunting or pursuing prey.

767.

Dingoes are known for their intelligence and problem-solving skills, often finding innovative ways to obtain food.

768.

They have a social hierarchy within their packs, with an alpha pair
leading and breeding while other members assist in raising young
and hunting.

769.

Dingoes have a breeding season typically occurring from autumn to
spring, with the female giving birth to a litter of pups after a
gestation period of around 63 days.

770.

The female builds a den in a secluded area, such as a cave or hollow
tree, to provide a safe and sheltered space for raising the pups.

771.

Dingoes exhibit monogamous mating behavior, with pairs typically
remaining together for life.

772.

Pups are born blind and rely on their mother's milk for the first few
weeks before transitioning to solid food.

773.

The survival rate of Dingo pups is relatively high, with both parents
and other pack members contributing to their care and protection.

774.

Dingoes have a unique method of communication called "play-
bowing," where they lower their front body while keeping their rear
end elevated, signaling their intention to play.

775.

The Dingoes' resilience and adaptability have allowed them to
survive in the Australian landscape for thousands of years.

776.

Despite being considered a wild species, Dingoes can interbreed with domestic dogs, leading to hybrid populations.

777.

Dingoes play an important ecological role as apex predators, helping to control populations of introduced species and maintain ecosystem balance.

778.

The status of the Dingo is subject to conservation concerns, as hybridization with domestic dogs and persecution by humans threaten their genetic integrity and survival.

779.

Indigenous Australian cultures have long-standing connections with Dingoes, considering them significant spiritual and cultural symbols.

780.

Dingoes have been depicted in ancient Aboriginal rock art, emphasizing their cultural and historical significance.

781.

Some studies suggest that Dingoes may have an impact on reducing populations of feral cats and foxes, which are responsible for the decline of several native Australian species.

782.

Dingoes are excellent swimmers and have been observed crossing bodies of water, such as rivers or channels, to access new territories or food sources.

783.

In some regions, Dingoes have been employed as a natural form of
pest control, helping to manage populations of invasive species.

784.

Dingoes have adapted to living in close proximity to human
settlements, where they may scavenge from garbage or prey on
livestock, leading to conflicts with farmers.

785.

The ecological role of Dingoes has led to debates about their
conservation status, with some advocating for their protection as a
native species, while others view them as pests or threats to
livestock.

786.

The Australian government has implemented various management
strategies to address conflicts between Dingoes and human activities,
including the use of exclusion fences, livestock guardian animals,
and targeted control measures.

787.

Dingoes have a strong bite force, which helps them to subdue and
kill their prey quickly.

788.

They are skilled diggers and can create extensive burrows or dens in
the ground for shelter or breeding purposes.

789.

Dingoes have adapted to the arid and semi-arid regions of Australia,
where they can survive with limited water resources by obtaining
moisture from their prey.

790.

The Dingo is protected in some parts of Australia, such as national parks, to preserve its genetic purity and ecological role.

791.

The presence of Dingoes in certain ecosystems has been associated with increased biodiversity and the preservation of native flora and fauna.

792.

Dingoes have a keen sense of hearing, enabling them to detect prey or potential threats even from a considerable distance.

793.

In Aboriginal mythology and folklore, Dingoes are often portrayed as significant and revered figures, representing spiritual and cultural values.

794.

Dingoes have been the subject of scientific research to better understand their behavior, genetics, and ecological interactions.

795.

The Dingo's sense of smell is highly developed, allowing them to locate hidden or buried food sources.

796.

The Dingo's coat is well-suited for the Australian climate, providing insulation during colder periods and reflecting heat during hot summers.

797.

Dingoes are known to display a range of vocalizations, including barks, howls, growls, and yips, each serving a different communicative purpose.

798.

Dingoes have a strong instinct for self-preservation, which helps them survive in challenging environments and avoid potential dangers.

799.

The population size of Dingoes in Australia is difficult to estimate accurately due to their wide distribution and varying degrees of hybridization.

800.

Dingoes are a symbol of Australia's unique wildlife heritage and are highly regarded by many for their intrinsic value and ecological significance.

801.

Apache Pass is a historically significant mountain pass located in southeastern Arizona, USA.

802.

The pass played a critical role in the movement of people, goods, and military forces throughout the American Southwest.

803.

It served as a natural corridor for various Native American tribes, including the Apache, Navajo, and O'odham, who used it for trade and travel.

804.

Apache Pass gained strategic importance during the Apache Wars in the late 19th century, as it provided access to the heartland of the Chiricahua Apache.

805.

Fort Bowie was established in 1862 near Apache Pass as a U.S. Army outpost to protect settlers and travelers from Apache raids.

806.

The fort was named after Colonel George Washington Bowie, who was killed in action during the Mexican-American War.

807.

The soldiers stationed at Fort Bowie faced frequent clashes with the Apache, including famous leaders such as Cochise and Geronimo.

808.

The Battle of Apache Pass, fought in 1862, was a significant engagement between the Union Army and the Confederate Army during the American Civil War.

809.

The Butterfield Overland Mail route, an important stagecoach line connecting the East and West coasts, passed through Apache Pass.

810.

Fort Bowie was abandoned in 1894, but the site was preserved and designated as a National Historic Site in 1964.

811.

The remains of several adobe and stone buildings can still be seen at the Fort Bowie site, providing a glimpse into the past.

812.

The fort's location near water sources made it strategically important for both military and civilian purposes.

813.

Apache Pass and Fort Bowie became known as a focal point for conflict and negotiation between Native Americans, settlers, and the U.S. government.

814.

The Apache Pass Trail, a hiking trail that follows the historic route through the pass, allows visitors to experience the landscape and history firsthand.

815.

The area surrounding Apache Pass is rich in natural beauty, with rugged mountains, scenic vistas, and diverse flora and fauna.

816.

The site serves as a reminder of the complex and often violent history of the American Southwest, highlighting the struggles and resilience of various cultures.

817.

Archaeological excavations at Apache Pass have unearthed artifacts and structures that provide valuable insights into the daily lives of soldiers and Native Americans.

818.

The Chiricahua Apache used Apache Pass as a strategic stronghold and a base for launching raids on settlements and military outposts.

819.

The Battle of Apache Pass in 1862 resulted in a Union victory and played a role in securing the Southwest for the Union during the Civil War.

820.

The Apache Wars, which took place from the 1850s to the 1880s, were a series of conflicts between the United States and various Apache tribes, with Apache Pass serving as a key battleground.

821.

The Apache Pass region has significant cultural and spiritual importance to Native American tribes, who continue to have strong connections to the land.

822.

The Fort Bowie National Historic Site features a visitor center that provides exhibits, educational programs, and interpretive displays about the history of the area.

823.

The trail to Fort Bowie passes through beautiful desert landscapes, offering opportunities for wildlife viewing and nature appreciation.

824.

The ruins of a Butterfield Stage Station can also be found along the trail, providing a glimpse into the transportation networks of the 19th century.

825.

Visitors to Apache Pass can explore the remains of Apache Spring, a vital water source that sustained both soldiers and Native Americans.

826.

The rugged terrain and strategic location of Apache Pass made it difficult for military forces to control the area effectively.

827.

The military presence at Fort Bowie played a role in shaping the settlement and development of the surrounding region.

828.

The conflicts at Apache Pass were not limited to military engagements but also involved negotiations, diplomacy, and cultural exchanges.

829.

The Chiricahua Apache leader Cochise had a complex relationship with Fort Bowie, at times engaging in negotiations and at other times leading attacks against the fort.

830.

Fort Bowie was a significant logistical hub for military operations in the region, supplying troops and materials for various campaigns.

831.

The Apache Pass area is known for its rich biodiversity, with numerous plant and animal species adapted to the arid desert environment.

832.

The surrounding mountain ranges, such as the Chiricahua Mountains, offer opportunities for hiking, birdwatching, and exploring unique geological formations.

833.

The area is also home to archaeological sites that provide evidence of human occupation dating back thousands of years.

834.

Apache Pass has been the subject of research and study by historians, archaeologists, and anthropologists, shedding light on the region's complex history.

835.

The nearby Chiricahua National Monument showcases stunning rock formations and offers recreational activities such as camping and scenic drives.

836.

The Apache Pass area has a rich military history, serving as a stage for conflicts between Native American tribes, European settlers, and the U.S. Army.

837.

The Apache Pass Trail provides an opportunity for visitors to retrace the footsteps of those who traveled through the pass in the past.

838.

The rugged beauty of the landscape surrounding Apache Pass has inspired artists, writers, and photographers over the years.

839.

The site serves as a memorial to the soldiers and Native Americans who fought and died in the conflicts of the American Southwest.

840.

Apache Pass and Fort Bowie are listed on the National Register of Historic Places, recognizing their historical and cultural significance.

841.

The area offers a unique blend of natural and cultural attractions, making it an appealing destination for outdoor enthusiasts and history buffs alike.

842.

The ruins of Fort Bowie provide a tangible connection to the past, allowing visitors to imagine life on the frontier during a turbulent period in American history.

843.

The stories and legends associated with Apache Pass have been passed down through generations, contributing to the cultural heritage of the region.

844.

The military operations at Fort Bowie and Apache Pass were part of a larger effort to control and pacify the American West during the expansion of the United States.

845.

The landscape of Apache Pass has witnessed the movements of indigenous peoples, Spanish explorers, Mexican settlers, and American pioneers.

846.

The area is known for its dark skies, offering excellent opportunities for stargazing and astronomical observations.

847.

The rugged terrain and hidden canyons around Apache Pass provided ideal hiding places for outlaws and renegade groups in the Old West.

848.

The Apache Pass region has been immortalized in literature, including works by renowned authors such as Willa Cather and Zane Grey.

849.

The ruins of Fort Bowie and the surrounding area provide a tangible link to the past, reminding us of the challenges and triumphs of those who came before us.

850.

Apache Pass continues to be a site of historical and cultural significance, attracting visitors who seek to explore its natural beauty and learn about its rich heritage.

851.

Awatovi Ruins is an archaeological site located in northeastern Arizona, USA.

852.

The ruins were once the site of a large pueblo inhabited by the Ancestral Puebloans, specifically the Hopi people.

853.

The pueblo was constructed around 1300 CE and was occupied for several centuries.

854.

Awatovi was one of the largest and most influential communities in the region during its time.

855.

The name "Awatovi" translates to "place of pottery" in the Hopi language, indicating the importance of pottery production in the community.

856.

The ruins consist of multiple structures, including kivas (ceremonial chambers), living quarters, and storage rooms.

857.

The architecture of Awatovi reflects the unique building techniques and styles of the Ancestral Puebloans.

858.

The pueblo was strategically located near water sources and agricultural fields, allowing the inhabitants to sustain their community.

859.

Awatovi was a hub for trade and exchange, as evidenced by the presence of exotic artifacts from distant regions.

860.

The ruins provide valuable insights into the social, economic, and religious practices of the Ancestral Puebloans.

861.

Excavations at Awatovi have uncovered numerous artifacts, including pottery, stone tools, and ceremonial items.

862.

The ruins also contain a large number of murals and rock art, depicting various aspects of daily life, rituals, and symbolism.

863.

Awatovi had extensive connections with other pueblo communities in the region, as well as with Mesoamerican cultures to the south.

864.

The pueblo was a center for learning and knowledge, attracting scholars, artists, and religious leaders from neighboring communities.

865.

The site was abandoned in the late 17th century, likely due to conflicts and social upheaval in the region.

866.

The reasons for the abandonment of Awatovi remain a subject of debate among archaeologists and historians.

867.

The ruins were rediscovered in the early 20th century and have since been the focus of extensive archaeological research.

868.

The preservation of Awatovi Ruins is of great importance, as it provides a window into the history and culture of the Ancestral Puebloans.

869.

The site is listed on the National Register of Historic Places and is considered a significant cultural and archaeological resource.

870.

Awatovi Ruins offer visitors the opportunity to explore the remains of an ancient pueblo and learn about the lives of its inhabitants.

871.

The ruins are located within the boundaries of the Hopi Reservation and hold spiritual and cultural significance for the Hopi people.

872.

Guided tours and interpretive programs are available to visitors, providing a deeper understanding of the site's history and cultural context.

873.

Awatovi Ruins have been a subject of study and research for archaeologists interested in understanding the dynamics of prehistoric pueblo societies.

874.

The architecture of the pueblo reflects the advanced engineering skills of the Ancestral Puebloans, who built multi-story structures with intricate masonry.

875.

The murals found at Awatovi Ruins depict various aspects of religious ceremonies, celestial events, and daily life activities.

876.

The site is believed to have been an important ceremonial center, where rituals and ceremonies took place.

877.

The presence of ceremonial objects and sacred symbols at Awatovi suggests that it held a special spiritual significance for the Ancestral Puebloans.

878.

The ruins provide evidence of long-distance trade networks, as artifacts from as far as Mexico have been found at the site.

879.

The strategic location of Awatovi allowed its inhabitants to control important trade routes and establish economic dominance in the region.

880.

The abandonment of Awatovi is believed to be related to internal conflicts among different factions within the pueblo.

881.

The ruins have undergone extensive stabilization and preservation efforts to protect them from erosion and further degradation.

882.

Awatovi Ruins have been a site of ongoing research, with archaeologists uncovering new insights about the Ancestral Puebloan culture.

883.

The presence of human remains at the site has provided valuable information about ancient burial practices and funerary rituals.

884.

Excavations at Awatovi have revealed evidence of violence and warfare, shedding light on the complex social dynamics of the time.

885.

The ruins are surrounded by a beautiful natural landscape, offering visitors the opportunity to appreciate the scenic beauty of the region.

886.

Awatovi Ruins are part of the wider archaeological landscape of the American Southwest, which includes other significant pueblo sites.

887.

The site provides a glimpse into the daily lives of the Ancestral Puebloans, from their agricultural practices to their pottery-making techniques.

888.

The ruins are located in an area rich in archaeological sites, allowing visitors to explore the broader historical context of the region.

889.

The cultural significance of Awatovi extends beyond its archaeological value, as it holds important spiritual meaning for the Hopi people.

890.

The ruins have been featured in various scholarly publications, contributing to the understanding of Ancestral Puebloan culture and history.

891.

Awatovi Ruins have been a site of collaboration between archaeologists and the Hopi Tribe, ensuring that the cultural heritage is respected and protected.

892.

The architecture of Awatovi showcases the ingenuity and skill of the Ancestral Puebloans in constructing complex multi-story buildings without modern tools.

893.

The pueblo's layout and organization suggest a hierarchical social structure, with different rooms and areas serving specific functions.

894.

The ruins have provided evidence of specialized craft production, including pottery-making, weaving, and stone tool manufacturing.

895.

The artifacts found at Awatovi reflect the exchange of goods and ideas among different cultures, highlighting the interconnectedness of ancient societies.

896.

The site offers visitors a glimpse into the challenges and adaptations of the Ancestral Puebloans in coping with a harsh desert environment.

897.

Awatovi Ruins serve as a reminder of the resilience and cultural richness of the indigenous peoples who inhabited the American Southwest.

898.

The ruins have inspired artistic and literary works, serving as a muse for writers, painters, and photographers.

899.

The preservation and interpretation of Awatovi Ruins contribute to the broader understanding of human history and cultural diversity.

900.

The site is a testament to the enduring legacy of the Ancestral Puebloans and their contributions to the cultural tapestry of the American Southwest.

901.

John Marshall was born on September 24, 1755, in Germantown, Virginia (now Midland, Virginia).

902.

He was the fourth Chief Justice of the United States, serving from 1801 until his death in 1835.

903.

Marshall is widely regarded as one of the most influential Supreme Court justices in American history.

904.

He played a crucial role in shaping the doctrine of judicial review, establishing the Supreme Court as the final authority on interpreting the Constitution.

905.

Marshall was a Federalist and a strong advocate for a strong central government.

906.

He served as the Secretary of State under President John Adams before being appointed as Chief Justice by President Adams.

907.

Marshall presided over many landmark Supreme Court cases, including Marbury v. Madison, McCulloch v. Maryland, and Gibbons v. Ogden.

908.

He authored the majority opinion in Marbury v. Madison, which established the principle of judicial review.

909.

Marshall's decisions on the Supreme Court consistently upheld the power of the federal government and strengthened the authority of the Constitution.

910.

He played a key role in defining the relationship between the federal and state governments, asserting federal supremacy in matters of national importance.

911.

Marshall was known for his keen legal mind and eloquent writing style, which made his opinions highly influential and persuasive.

912.

He helped establish the principle that the Constitution is a living document that should adapt to changing circumstances and societal needs.

913.

Marshall's decisions often sought to promote economic growth and development, supporting policies that encouraged interstate commerce and federal infrastructure projects.

914.

He was involved in resolving disputes between Native American tribes and the United States government, often favoring federal authority over tribal rights.

915.

Marshall's decisions helped shape the concept of tribal sovereignty and the legal status of Native American nations.

916.

He was a staunch defender of property rights and believed in the importance of protecting private property from government encroachment.

917.

Marshall's decisions on contract law and property rights laid the groundwork for modern commercial and business law.

918.

He was an advocate for a strong and independent judiciary, believing that it was necessary to safeguard the rights and liberties of individuals.

919.

Marshall's jurisprudence emphasized the importance of a strong national government in promoting stability, order, and unity.

920.

He played a critical role in settling disputes between states, helping to maintain the balance of power within the federal system.

921.

Marshall's legal opinions were often characterized by a pragmatic and practical approach, seeking to find workable solutions to complex legal issues.

922.

He was known for his commitment to fairness, impartiality, and the rule of law, even when his decisions went against his personal beliefs.

923.

Marshall's influence extended beyond his time on the Supreme Court, as his decisions continue to shape constitutional interpretation to this day.

924.

He was a strong advocate for the independence of the judiciary and believed in the importance of checks and balances in a democratic society.

925.

Marshall's legal philosophy emphasized the need for a strong central government to protect individual rights and maintain national unity.

926.

He was a respected and admired figure in his time, known for his integrity, intellect, and dedication to public service.

927.

Marshall's decisions helped establish the Supreme Court as a co-equal branch of government alongside the executive and legislative branches.

928.

He was instrumental in defining the limits of state power and the extent of federal authority, creating a framework for the federal system that still exists today.

929.

Marshall's legacy extends beyond his legal career, as he was also involved in politics, serving in the Virginia House of Delegates and the U.S. House of Representatives.

930.

He was a strong advocate for religious freedom and believed in the separation of church and state, as reflected in his opinions on cases involving religious liberties.

931.

Marshall was a proponent of strong national defense and supported the expansion of the military during his time as Chief Justice.

932.

He was involved in international diplomacy, serving as a peace commissioner during negotiations with France and Great Britain.

933.

Marshall was a lifelong learner and avid reader, constantly expanding his knowledge of law, history, and philosophy.

934.

He had a reputation for being reserved and dignified, earning him the nickname "The Great Chief Justice."

935.

Marshall was known for his sense of humor, often using wit and satire in his legal opinions to make his points more effectively.

936.

He was married to Mary Willis Ambler, and they had ten children together.

937.

Marshall's childhood home in Virginia, known as the John Marshall House, is now a museum and historic site.

938.

He was deeply committed to public service and believed in the importance of upholding the principles of the Constitution.

939.

Marshall's decisions on the Supreme Court were not always unanimous, and he faced criticism and dissent from other justices.

940.

He was a mentor to many aspiring lawyers and judges, providing guidance and advice on legal matters.

941.

Marshall was a prolific writer, and his opinions and speeches continue to be studied and analyzed by legal scholars and students.

942.

He had a strong sense of duty and responsibility, often sacrificing personal interests for the greater good.

943.

Marshall's decisions helped establish the supremacy of federal law over state law, ensuring uniformity and consistency in the interpretation of the Constitution.

944.

He was a strong advocate for the rights of individuals, including the right to a fair trial and the protection against unreasonable searches and seizures.

945.

Marshall's legal career spanned over three decades, making him one of the longest-serving Chief Justices in U.S. history.

946.

He believed in the power of education and served as a trustee for several educational institutions, including the College of William & Mary.

947.

Marshall's contributions to American jurisprudence have been recognized and honored with numerous awards and accolades.

948.

He was known for his deep knowledge of constitutional law and his ability to apply legal principles to complex and challenging cases.

949.

Marshall's decisions helped shape the interpretation of the Commerce Clause of the Constitution, which grants the federal government the power to regulate interstate commerce.

He was involved in the drafting of Georgia's first state constitution in 1777 and later served as a member of the Georgia Constitutional Convention in 1789.

966.

McIntosh's political career was not as successful as his military endeavors, and he faced significant opposition and criticism from his rivals.

967.

He was a supporter of the Yazoo land sales, which led to a major political scandal and controversy in Georgia during the 1790s.

968.

McIntosh's role in the Yazoo land fraud weakened his political standing and contributed to his eventual retirement from public life.

969.

He lived out his later years in Georgia, engaging in agriculture and land speculation to support his family.

970.

McIntosh was involved in promoting settlement and development in the Georgia frontier, helping to establish new communities and infrastructure.

971.

He had a mixed reputation among his contemporaries, with some admiring his military prowess and others criticizing his temperament and political choices.

972.

McIntosh's descendants continued to play influential roles in Georgia's political and military history, with several notable figures among his lineage.

973.

He was known for his colorful and expressive language, often employing vivid and memorable phrases in his speeches and writings.

974.

McIntosh was a dedicated patriot who believed deeply in the cause of American independence and the principles of liberty.

975.

He was of mixed heritage, with his mother being of Creek and Scottish descent and his father of Scottish ancestry.

976.

McIntosh's diverse background gave him a unique perspective on the relationships between European settlers and Native American tribes.

977.

He was involved in negotiations and treaties with Native American nations, striving for peaceful coexistence and fair treatment.

978.

McIntosh's military career was not limited to the Revolutionary War; he also fought against the British in the War of 1812.

979.

He served as a brigadier general in the Georgia militia during the War of 1812, defending the state against British invasion.

980.

McIntosh's leadership during the War of 1812 earned him respect and recognition from his fellow officers and soldiers.

981.

He was a member of the Freemasons, a fraternal organization that played a prominent role in the social and political life of the time.

982.

McIntosh's legacy is commemorated through various landmarks and institutions, including McIntosh County, Georgia, and McIntosh Academy, a high school in Darien, Georgia.

983.

He died on February 20, 1806, in Savannah, Georgia, at the age of 80.

984.

McIntosh's final resting place is in Colonial Park Cemetery in Savannah, where a monument honors his contributions to American history.

985.

His life and career continue to be studied and analyzed by historians, offering insights into the complexities of the Revolutionary War era.

986.

McIntosh's story reflects the challenges and complexities faced by many military and political leaders during the tumultuous years of the American Revolution.

987.

He left behind a legacy of courage, determination, and a commitment to the principles of liberty and self-governance.

988.

McIntosh's experiences as a frontiersman and his interactions with Native American tribes contributed to his broader understanding of the complexities of American expansion and settlement.

989.

He was well-respected for his military expertise and tactical skills, often relied upon by his superiors for his strategic advice.

990.

McIntosh's military campaigns in the southern colonies helped secure vital territories and disrupt British control in the region.

991.

He was known for his personal bravery and fearlessness on the battlefield, leading by example and inspiring his troops.

992.

McIntosh's efforts to defend Georgia's interests during the Revolutionary War were instrumental in securing the state's participation in the newly formed United States.

993.

He had a strong commitment to the principles of self-determination and liberty, advocating for the rights of the individual and the preservation of democratic values.

994.

McIntosh's involvement in the Yazoo land controversy brought him into conflict with powerful political opponents, straining his reputation and limiting his political influence.

995.

He was a proponent of agrarian society, believing in the importance of agriculture and land ownership for economic and political stability.

996.

McIntosh's military successes in the Revolutionary War helped establish his reputation as a capable and effective leader.

997.

He was known for his quick thinking and adaptability on the battlefield, often making strategic decisions that turned the tide of battle.

998.

McIntosh's commitment to the principles of self-government and popular sovereignty was reflected in his political actions and writings.

999.

He was an influential figure in shaping Georgia's early political landscape, advocating for a strong state government and protection of individual rights.

1000.

McIntosh's contributions to the American Revolution and the founding of the United States are commemorated and celebrated as part of the nation's history and heritage.